GW01458154

The
SavvyGuide To

HPC, GRID, DATA GRID, VIRTUALISATION AND CLOUD COMPUTING

Adam Vile and Jim Liddle

AUTHORS: Adam Vile and Jim Liddle

Published by The SavvyGuideTo LTD 2009

ISBN 978-0-9559907-0-0

Copyright © 2009 The SavvyGuideTo. All rights reserved. No part of this book may be copied for any use other than personal use, without the express permission of one of the authors.

Acknowledgements

It takes time and energy to write a book like this, time and energy that we could be spending with our families and friends. We would like to first and foremost thank them for putting up with the fact that we haven't been there as much as we could. Adam would like to thank to Zoe and Matthew for giving him space and time to think and for letting me use the computer, and Jim would like to thank his wonderful wife Ana for putting up with him spending his evenings writing this book.

There are many people in the technology world that we have rubbed shoulder with, learnt from and bounced ideas off of. We would like to thank them, there are of course too many to name but you know who you are.

Our special thanks go to friends and colleagues who have contributed to this book either by kick-starting thinking or feeding back on content, chapters and ideas: Stephen Deakin, Lewis Foti, Kamran Yousaf, Nati Shalom and Steve Colwell

Contents

Introduction

There was a time when a single computer, with vacuum tubes, crystal diodes and hand soldered joints, filled an entire room and could carry out almost 5000 additions every second. We have come a long way since then. As a conservative estimate, the hand held games console that my children use has a hundred times the computational power of that computer, and my mobile phone has more computational power than the NASA computers that sent a man to the moon. As computers get more compact, you might expect that the space they occupy decreases. However, this has not exactly been the pattern.

The problem is that even though the size of computers has reduced exponentially according to Moores law, the demand for computational resource has increased super exponentially. This is the Easter egg syndrome - it doesn't matter how big an Easter egg I give to my children, they will always want more (the very fact that I can give them a really big egg confirms this for them!!). Computational resource has proved its use in first military, then commercial and finally home applications, and for most of us a really fast chip means that we can render web pages or play games faster. But the millions of desktop and laptop CPU's around the world are not where we find the real requirements for faster and more compute. It is demand for more accuracy, more throughput and higher volumes of computations in areas such as weather prediction, measurement of financial risk, design of racing cars and aeroplane components.

These application areas have two things in common: massive amounts of computation are required to get meaningful results; and the need for speed. It is no good having a meaningful weather report if it is two days late for example, and banks have requirements to submit risk reports on hundreds of thousands of positions daily. Specialist solutions are required to provide the amount of compute that are needed to address these problems, but these solutions do not come cheap. A combination of computer science, government funding and commerce has fuelled design and construction of High Performance and High Throughput systems from specialist hardware, through supercomputers and clusters to grid systems.

In this book we take HPC to mean 'High Performance Computing'. This may seem to be stating the obvious, but HPC is also beginning to gather pace as an acronym for 'High Productivity Computing' which brings together HPC, Grid, DataGrid, and virtualisation (of Middleware, storage and OS). High Performance Computing systems and environments typically use large numbers of processors, either as part of a single machine, or multiple computers that are organised in a cluster that operate as a single computing resource. HPC has always been expensive, often prohibitively so.

High-performance networking interconnects are used for cluster based HPC systems. InfiniBand or Myrinet are an example of such interconnects. The network topology for such systems tends to be either a simple bus topology or (for extreme HPC requirements) a mesh topology. Mesh topologies tend to provide lower latency between each of the hosts. Networking performance and transfer rates are therefore improved.

For a while the evolution of supercomputing was through such hardware, from scalar to vector processors, but the advent of parallel processing, coupled with advances in distributed systems and relatively cheap commodity hardware has made cluster and grid computing possible for most commercial organisations. This in turn has driven the development of enabling software, and in particular the introduction of significantly higher resilience and scalability features driven by the stringent requirements of the commercial environment. Grid is not strictly High Performance Computing, but it has enabled the concepts embodied in HPC to become mainstream.

The HPC domain is becoming software focused. There are two good reasons for this trend. The first is commoditisation of X86 architectures and the development of blade technology has enabled denser packing and better locality of reference than ever before, this hardware offers simple and cost effective maintenance and well known and understood programming models. The second is the abstraction of the software from the hardware architecture. Service oriented architecture and common API's and libraries ensure that applications are disconnected from hardware and software solutions and avoid the risk of lock-in whilst creating a scalable component based architecture.

Grid computing, from a technology perspective, is still relatively new, which is why skill-sets in this area are still valued at a premium. Grid enables massively scaled architectures and brings with it a host of organisational as well as technical challenges. Grid has the potential to drive up utilisation from less than 20% to nearer 70% on shared infrastructures, but although the technology exists the sharing of resources across organisational boundaries is not an easy thing to achieve.

Grid computing brings the flexibility of using standard non-heterogeneous hardware and standard operating systems, in which nodes can be added on demand. A standard software layer is applied across this infrastructure to achieve this. Key to the whole grid proposition is that dedicated computing resources are not necessary, which leads to many grids being built by reusing existing hardware to produce a powerful unified computing resource.

No special networking components are needed for grid, and grid computing is not limited to the local LAN. It is not unusual for MAN and WAN boundaries to be crossed when building a grid resource.

A grid can be thought of as a general computing resource in which different nodes of the grid work, in parallel, on computational tasks that have been broken down by the grid management software and farmed out using the grid scheduler. Unlike traditional HPC solutions each node can be working on different computational algorithms and tasks which, after being farmed out, are brought back together to calculate the final result.

A good example of this in practice is in Investment bank where grids are used to run Monte Carlo simulations to calculate risk. With the adoption of grid these types of calculations can now be run in near real-time allowing the banks to calculate risk positions on the fly which ultimately leads to shorter time to market, greater volumes and therefore increased revenue.

A simple example that illustrates this is SETI, the Search for Extraterrestrial Intelligence. The SETI at home project searches for transmissions from 'other' civilizations by analyse transmissions of cosmic origins to find patterns of communication. Clearly this is a vast undertaking and would require a practically infinite amount of compute resource. Cleverly the SETI project taps into the idle resources of millions of personal computers around the world for the analysis of raw SETI data. This is done by farming out work to home user PCs that have installed a SETI screen saver. They analyse a chunk of work when idle and send the data result back, functioning very much like a vast on-demand geographically dispersed grid, albeit one that has no latency constraints or end goal in sight!

As compute architectures scale then a new problem arises, data movement. The questions that many owners of large grids are now asking are: *How do we get the data and the computational task on the same compute node? How do we share common data across thousands of nodes? How do we ensure consistency of data in a real time environment when such latency is involved at such scale?* Databases and shared file systems are woefully inadequate in this high performance, high scale, high throughput environment and so data cache technologies are being employed along with parallel file systems to address these new requirements.

Commoditisation has created massive physical installed bases which have enormous power and cooling requirements. There is one bank for example; whose London data center draws more power in a day than the city of Manchester. There is no solution, other than perhaps building data centers in Siberia next to a nuclear power station; we have to find ways of generating more compute with less power demands. HPC hardware has recently become a topic of interest as it offers local parallelism and potentially large shared memories at very low cost of power. A useful fact to remember is that if you halve the clock speed of a processor, you use a quarter of the power. You will not get quite so many instructions per second in serial, but what if you went from one 2GHz processor to two 1GHz processors and had a way of exploiting the parallelism?

Not every program or procedure is parallelisable. Amdahl's law, which we discuss in detail in a later chapter, gives a rule for the limits of parallelism in any given algorithm. Re-engineering and re-factoring code to take full advantage of HPC hardware requires effort and in a commercial setting the costs of this re-factoring may make HPC hardware less viable, at least in the short term. In the medium term it is inevitable that the processor density will increase and that multicore hardware will become commonplace. Code will be designed up front to take advantage of these developments and the rate at which we increase the heat, power and space requirements will be slowed, but is unlikely to stop.

Grid applications are typically compute oriented, and there are good speedups to be had in the initial stages of parallelising an application. However the problem soon shifts as the number of compute nodes increases, to one of moving any required data around quickly enough to ensure that the compute resources are fully utilised. We discuss this problem in the grid chapter. Data Grids can address this problem, and their applicability extends beyond this into many kinds of large scale distributed compute problem. In many ways Data Grid is a specialized used of grid for certain types of applications that traditionally were not considered suitable for grid.

Grid can be though of as a virtualisation technology. In fact the sales pitch for both grid and virtualisation is focussed around increasing utilisation and resource flexibility. One way of thinking about the difference is to see Grid as enabling many processors behave as one, and virtualisation enabling one processor to behave as many. Virtualisation is now mainstream technology for data center management and the economics certainly make sense.

One of the more recent developments in the HPC world is the rise of Cloud or utility computing. Cloud Computing is essentially distributed computing that is built using services distributed over multiple locations. The services are typically delivered using a Grid or a cluster as resource. Public Clouds are hosted by companies such as Amazon (an example being their EC2 offering) and private clouds are typically specialised offerings that organisations build which adopt the technologies and practices of public cloud infrastructures, albeit with additional security.

Grid, Data Grid and virtualisation combine in the Cloud paradigm to provide scalable resource pools that can be harnessed for test, development and production uses at scale. The aims of Cloud match closely the original vision for Grid, and a convergence is inevitable. Right now there are Clouds enabled through virtualisation technology, scheduled by a Grid workload manager, running applications build on Data Grids. This kind of configuration will become much more prevalent in the future.

Grid, Data Grid, HPC, Virtualisation and even Cloud technology are not new. These ideas and concepts have been developing in the academic context for over twenty years. Due to general requirements for more compute and better carbon footprint management interest in these technologies has been growing rapidly over the last five years. At this time, there are few technologists with detailed knowledge and exposure to these technologies in a commercial setting. There are a limited number of developers and architects who understand how to design and build systems and software that exploit these technologies, whilst at the same time addressing business needs, and there are fewer IT managers who have had the time to develop enough knowledge about the field to be able to make strategic decisions about the ways in which HPC, Grid and Data Grid fit into their future enterprise level hardware and software stacks.

The literature around these technologies is either focused on research and academia or is freely available in the form of vendor white-papers. The former are often obscure and not particularly relevant to the needs of business, the latter are designed as sales tools and as such offer a product centric view. This book offers an independent, consolidated overview of Grid, HPC, Data Grid, Virtualisation and Cloud as it relates to your business needs, and is put together in a way that will help you quickly understand the concepts, ideas, applications and issues around these technologies. It is designed to bridge the gap between theory and practice and is based upon our knowledge of implementing these technologies in practice in large and small organisations. It is aimed both at technical managers and decision makers who want to get an overview of the field and a review of the issues and current thinking, and at architects and developers who want to understand best practice for design and implementation of these technologies.

Each chapter is self-contained and contains and overview of each technology, a review of the current state of play, introducing the concepts and the main themes and highlighting the business and benefits of the various technologies. There is a focus on best practice and application and infrastructural patterns for exploiting these technologies in the business context. Each chapter contains a review of the available technologies and products for solving compute and data grid problems and draws on both vendor products and open source. There is an assumption here that in general off the shelf, pre-baked solutions will be cost effective ways of meeting your needs, and we specifically focus on tools that are readily available on the market. We aim to give you an understanding of the concepts, ideas and tools available now and equip you for future decision making.

THE BUSINESS DRIVERS

There are two reasons why grid and associated computing technologies have emerged as essential in today's data-centers – the first is business enablement and the second cost containment. We will deal with cost containment first, as business enablement is the more straightforward.

Cost containment

Compute estates of profitable companies in all sectors are

growing at unsustainable rates. Limitations are not space, but power and cooling. In the mid 2000's the major chip vendors were focused on increases in processor clock-speed and it became standard to have a minimum of a 3GHz processor in a server or desktop machine. If you have ever looked at over-clocking your PC, you will know that you need to buy the biggest fan possible to ensure that the chip does not melt, in a data center with chips running at or near peak, fans are not always big enough, and other alternatives such a air conditioning and water cooling are often employed. In Alaskan and Icelandic data centers, in the winter they just open the windows!! This means that the running costs far outweighs the purchase and depreciation costs of a data center resident computer, perhaps as much as 8 times over its lifetime.

We can have a quick look at a simple model hardware growth that takes into account the relevant factors, you can add your own numbers around this to come up with a cost model that makes sense in your organisation. First of all let us make some assumptions. Let us assume a linear growth (conservative at best) with a gradient of 2 (that is that the compute requirement increases by a factor of 2 every year) and that there are say 500 computers in place by the end of the first year. Let us also assume that utilisation is low, perhaps as low as 30% and that if we implement a grid solution which allows us to consolidate resource and increase utilisation, realistically perhaps to double it to 60%. We expect Moore's law to hold (that processer speed will double every 18 months) and we recognise that multicore technology will double the effective compute capability without increasing the number of physical machines (or the power requirements) at least once in over the three year period.

If none of these assumptions hold, we would have 2000 computers at the end of three years. If we introduce the multi-core assumption we would have 1250 (since we are not replacing any computers in this 3 year period, only new computers will be multi-core). Moore's law again only applies to computers purchased after the first 18 months and so has little effect. Introducing grid however reduces the effective estate to 760 computers.

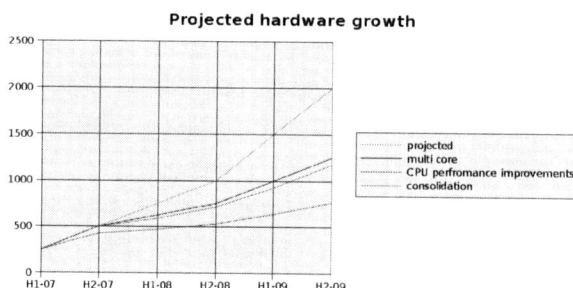

Projected hardware growth

Figure 1

These sums are much more impressive if we multiply the expected compute requirements by a factor of 10, which mirrors the current expectation in investment banks. There is therefore a significant case for both grid and the introduction and exploitation of multi-core (which is the remit of HPC) on the basis of cost containment. We could factor in additional utilisation savings (perhaps 10%) through the use of data cache technology, and perhaps even further savings through introducing virtualisation.

Cloud Computing will have a big impact on cost containment for Grid Computing as it offers an SaaS[1] pay-on-demand model that can work out at less than a dollar a grid enabled compute resource. The economics behind the offering are pretty straight forward. Take the cost of a server, lets say $3000, and amortizing it over 3 years means that the server needs to generate $1000 per year for break even. Add into this, power costs, cooling costs, High Availability options etc and you have a model where an hourly charge works out at around the $1 per

---

[1] SaaS – Software As A Service

hour we mentioned earlier. The ability to purchase compute cycles as a cheap resource without worrying about infrastructure, availability etc is very attractive and we will see Cloud Computing forming an essential part of a companies operating plan as well as it spawning new business opportunities. We will explore this aspect of Cloud Computing in greater detail later in the book

Business Enablement

Simply put, if the business have more compute they can do more and have the capability of making more money ("and more mistakes" you may say[2]). For the investment banker, more compute means faster and more accurate pricing and risking and essentially more operating capital to use for trading. Take for example a spreadsheet based option-pricer which takes a day to run on a trader desktop. When put onto a grid of 100 machines it may take a matter of minutes. This opens up the possibility of trading this instrument and making previously unavailable profit, all the better is if you can do this before other banks, this is your market edge.

In the pharmaceutical industry, being able to carry out drug simulations more rapidly and with more accuracy reduces time to market and increases profitability. The semiconductor industry use grid technology in their chip design process and will benefit from getting to market quicker.

Grids are good for computationally intensive type of applications with fixed sizes of data to work on. These data elements form the input to the computation tasks and tend to be small. However grids have been so successful in reducing TCO and ROA that it

---

[2] It could be conjectured that the recent credit crunch would not have been as bad if the traders had not been trading quite as complex instruments. These instruments are difficult to price and risk, and their use was only made possible by the provision of massive amounts of compute.

makes perfect sense to see what other type of applications they could be used for, and we will be discussing how the first generation of grid are evolving and utilising data and virtualisation to target different business areas.

It is easy to make a case for HPC, Grid and Data Cache technology on the grounds that it enables the business to be more competitive (or just to compete) , to manage risk better, and to increase the quality and timeliness of their product. Business units are always pushing for more results, faster. These technologies, if exploited correctly, can ensure that.

Summary

The value that HPC, Grid, Cloud and Virtualization technologies bring to companies means that their use of such technologies will continue to grow in the coming years. In fact many Telecommunications companies are now offering their own SaaS[3] applications and services.

We feel that HPC, Grid and Virtualisation have now crossed the chasm, evident by their ready adoption by mainstream enterprises. Cloud is growing as a concept and it is only a matter of time, driven by competitiveness and economies *at* scale, that it too leaps the chasm.

There is an increasing likelihood that you will come across one of HPC, Grid, Data Grid, Virtualisation or Cloud technologies in your organisation. After reading this book you should be well placed to not only understand such technologies but also have a view on how they could be used or applied.

---

[3] See the Cloud computing Chapter for definition of SaaS

Introducing HPC

The mention of High Performance Computing (HPC) may evoke images of bearded academics and IBM-ers standing around large noisy, hot, supercomputers lovingly named after characters from Lord of the Rings, as they crunch numbers for days on end trying to find the next biggest prime number. Of course, as with all stereotypes, there is a strong basis for this view but HPC has evolved from those halcyon days, where government funding was the only way to get enough cash to own and manage a supercomputer into something slightly different.

High Performance Computing refers to computing systems and environments that typically use large numbers of processors, either as part of a single machine, or multiple computers that are organised in a cluster that operate as a single computing resource.

HPC, both by necessity and by Darwinian selection, has embraced a commodity model enabled by message passing, grid and clustering technology that sits alongside specialist hardware design. It is a combination of both software and hardware stacks that create the High Performance Computing solutions today, in this chapter we will look at both of these elements introducing terms, concepts and ideas that are relevant for those wishing to understand HPC as it is today and as it may be in the future.

HPC business uses include data warehouses, line-of-business (LOB) applications and HPC provides the infrastructure for heavy transaction processing systems.

THE COMMODITISATION OF HPC

It has long been known[4] that because of the rate of improvements in chip design and performance, supercomputers become obsolete as soon as they are completed. In the past, the way to get more compute was to design specialist hardware that exploited concepts such as vector processing. The design and development of such hardware was costly, time consuming and usually required a supercomputer as an integral part of the design process.

Vector processors

A Vector processor is essentially a chip with the capability to carry out multiple calculations in parallel. There are two modes of operation that concern us here: Multiple Instructions Multiple Data (MIMD) which refers to the capability of the chip to carry out different instructions on different data in parallel streams and Single Instruction Multiple Data (SIMD) which is the capability of the chip to carry out the same instruction on different data in parallel. Consider a vector (1,2,3,4), a SIMD processor can only perform the same operation on each element:

```
par
Vector.Add(3)
end par
```

Resulting in (4,5,6,7). It would do this in a single clock cycle, which is much better than the 4 cycles it would take on a SISD processor (single instruction single data). A MIMD processor could however, perform the following set of operations:

```
par
Vector[0].Add(3)
Vector[1].Add(4)
```

---

[4] Kevin Dowd and Charles Severance (1998). High Performance Computing. O'Reiley

```
Vector[2].subtract(3)
Vector[3].mult(2)
End par
```

Resulting in (4,6,2,10). Again this would take place in one clock cycle. MIMD seems the most flexible approach, but flexibility comes at a cost and MIMD chips are more expensive to design and may not achieve such high clockspeeds. SIMD is practical in linear algebra (for example) in which multiple matrix and vector operations are required in parallel. Linear algebra is of course essential in any HPC application that requires the solution of Partial Differential Equations (PDE's). Weather simulations and fluid flow simulations, for example, require the numerical solution of PDE's. SIMD is also excellent for Monte Carlo simulations, as the number of parallel simulation paths is essentially equal to the number of elements in the vector.

Nowadays, vector processing is not only in the domain of supercomputers and standard chip manufacturers such as Intel include vector processing extensions (SSE) that can be exploited by programmers and compilers to gain significant speed-ups.

Case study – the Cell processor and Clearspeed CSX6000

Famously the Cell Broadband Engine found in the PlayStation 3 is a MIMD processor with 9 processing elements. This chip has been recently released in blade configuration by IBM giving the potential for 10 times speed-up over an Intel single code cpu. Since it was designed as an image processing engine, at the time of writing it supports single precision floating point arithmetic. However, there are plans to double the number of FPU's (floating point units) and make double precision available in hardware before the end of 2007.

The Clearspeed CSX6000 on the other hand is a 96-way SIMD processor. Each processing element runs at less than 300 MHZ and so this chip is extremely cool (less than 10Watts compared to the 75Watts of the standard X86 offerings), because of the massive degree of parallelism this chip can give up to 10 times speed-up (on the right sort of problem) against a standard X86 chip of about 2.8GHZ.

This brings us to the question of how to measure speed-up. This is a relatively over-used term and it is worthwhile here taking time to define it. Speed-up is essentially the ratio of the run time of the code under a baseline (perhaps on a single core processor) to the run time of the code under the "new" conditions. These conditions can be new compiler flags, new hardware or parallelisation, for example.

Clock speeds and multi-core

Another equally profitable approach to getting more compute is to cram more and more transistors onto a single piece of silicon. The physics of this works by reducing the distance needed to travel by a signal between gates and so a close packing means more transistors to carry out the operations and less communication time between them. Current chips are built on 65 nanometre silicone and certain chips are soon to emerge on 45 nanometre. This approach tends to increase the clock speed of the chips, which of course is desirable, but has a knock on effect in the requirements for cooling. A 1.5GHZ processor will actually emit four times less heat than a 3GHz processor, and so from the perspective of a carbon footprint, it is better to have four 1.5GHz processors than two 3GHZ processors.

This is exactly the approach taken by AMD and Intel in the creation of their multicore processors such as Barcelona (AMD) and Woodcrest (Intel). IBM have also adopted this approach for Bluegene which uses arrays of 64 750MHZ processors to build their Petaflop machine that sits at the top of the top 500 list. The problem with this approach is that code may have to be developed or modified to take advantage of multiple processors and multiple parallel execution streams. It is not uncommon in the world of HPC to make such code modifications, or even to design code and hardware architecture together to solve a specific problem (a good example of this is the forerunner of Bluegene, the QDOC machine, which was designed with protein folding calculations specifically in mind[5]).

Virtualisation is also having an effect on processors and processor design. Intel has recently launched the Xeon 7400 "Dunnington" processor family. The new chip series includes seven processors and the first six-core x86 processor. Platforms based on these processors can scale up to 16 processor "sockets" to deliver servers with up to 96 processing cores inside. he new Xeon® 7400 series delivers exceptional performance improvements with lower power consumption. The processor delivers almost 50 percent better performance, and up to 10 percent reduction in platform power. It has also resulted in a world record VMmark (a virtualization benchmark) score for four-socket, 24 processing core servers at 18.49 on a Dell PowerEdge R900 platform using VMware ESX server v3.5.0.

Memory access

Calculations require data, from the register, from the L1 or L2 cache, from the on board memory or from some memory or data store outside of the machine itself. I/O and memory access are sure ways of slowing down code and the main aims of any developer of software or compilers is to keep the ratio of memory access to compute as small as possible. It is good practice to ensure good locality of reference of data and computation. Hardware manufacturers continue to investigate ways of reducing memory access times, and have increased the sizes of

---

[5]http://www.icsa.inf.ed.ac.uk/research/groups/hase/projects/qcd/

caches considerably (the AMD Athlon has 512K of L2 cache) as well as introducing architectures designed to improve memory access in multicore systems.

AMD has integrated a NUMA (Non Uniform Memory Access) approach in their integrated memory controller which has enabled the CPU to access local RAM at very low latency and allows the Opteron chip to perform extremely well at lower clock speeds. Modern CPU's operate considerably faster than main memory and limits in the cache memory available cause CPU data starvation. In a multi core situation this problem becomes worse, with the potential to significantly effect saleability. The NUMA approach provides separate memory for each core, or processor, mitigating risk of contention where all cores require the same data at the same time and potentially increasing speed-up by up to a factor equal to the number of separate memory banks. The NUMA architecture was developed alongside symmetric multiprocessor systems.

SMP (Symmetric Multiprocessor systems)

Introduced in 1961, the Burroughs B5500 (REF) mainframe had many features including the ability to operate on a master-worker paradigm[6] and a virtual memory, This is an architecture where two or more identical processors are connected to a shared memory. Essentially this is the way that multicore CPU's are architected. The programming model for SMP is through running separate threads, sometimes one per processor, but often the choice of what runs where is left to the operating system. Since all CPU's share the same memory each thread can potentially require the same data consistently. Under a NUMA architecture this requires intelligent cache capability that ensures coherence and consistency amongst all memory units. This as always

---

[6] Discussed in the Grid chapter

means compromise - in this case between speed and consistency. SMP based systems have proved popular in the past as software can run without modification and, if already written in a thread compatible way, can exploit the inherent parallelism provided by the hardware through the operating system. SMP systems are ideal for databases, webservers and application server and they often form the basis of supercomputing, grid and cluster computing solutions.

Supercomputers

The top500 list, which gives a ranking of the top 500 fastest computers on the planet is published every six months [7]. The 'speed' of these computers is measured by running a High Performance LINPACK[8](HPL) test. This is a test that measures the execution rate of floating point arithmetic by running a programme that solves a set of linear equations. Underlying the Linpack test are the BLAS[9] libraries, which essentially makes the test available to any hardware that supports an implementation of these libraries. BLAS and LINPACK support a variety of data types and matrix sizes. HPL is a parallel implementation of the LINPACK algorithm and is suitable for running on any size of computer with any number of CPU's.

The Top 500 list

The Supercomputer world moves very fast, and the top performer at the time of writing (Nov 2008) is Roadrunner, an IBM Bladecentre cluster with a combination of Cell Processors AMD Opteron processors connected by Infiniband high-speed network. Altogether there are 129600 cores, although it is not

---

[7] The top 500 list is published at http://www.top500.org

[8] The Linpack benchmartk sourcecode is available at http://www.netlib.org/benchmark/

[9] BLAS, are a set of libraries for performing basic linear algebra.

clear how these are divided between the two-processor types. This cluster is designed for research, and is housed in the Los Alomos Laboratory in New Mexico. It is the first Peta-Flop computer, as it can carry out 1.456 Quadrillion floating point calculations per second. Not far behind is a Cray XT5 with a Linpack score of 1381400 G/Flops[10] or Linpack score of 1381.4 T/Flops (TerraFlops). This XT5 has 150,152 cores, whereas Roadrunner has only 129,600 demonstrating processor efficiency.

Roadrunner is almost three times faster than the computer that held the top place for over a year, BlueGene/L. This is a bespoke supercomputer, also manufactured by IBM. housed at the Lawrence Livermore Laboratory in California. It can run a measly can run 478.2 trillion calculations per second, having a Linpack score of 478.2 T/Flops (TerraFlops). Furthermore the Bluegene/L has 212992 processors, twice as many as roadrunner. There is a reason for this and it relates to a further consideration, which does not concern the top500 list but certainly concerns the owners of data centers, the FLOP/Watt statistic. Bluegene/L has an enormous amount of processors, each (a modified Power PC rev 4 processor) has two cores each running at 700Mhz, reducing the power draw by a factor of 8 per core over a 2.0 Ghz processor.

Given that the way of measuring a top performing Supercomputer is via the LINPACK test, it is obviously within manufacturers interests to design with a good architecture for LINPACK in mind. This does happen, and although computers with a good LINPACK result are not useless, it is always better to test against realistic applications, preferably the ones that are going to be run on the supercomputer. The SPEC HPG

---

[10] One FLOP is one floating point operation per second.

benchmarks[11] are designed to overcome this problem and performance of Supercomputers is measured by the time to run canonical applications taken from the Seismic, Chemical and Weather industries. This has resulted in an alternative list of the Top Application Performers (TAP)[12], on which a number of the top500 list Supercomputers do not feature, either because they have not been tested, or because they are not a Top Application Performer. The key differentiator of the SPEC HPG benchmarks is that they include a strict validation test, which tests the accuracy of the result. In some cases these tests are not passed by tested Supercomputers.

This highlights a very important point, which is that the computer system that you choose must be fit for purpose. Supercomputers condense a lot of CPU and memory into a smallish space and connect them all with fast communications links. In order to achieve this efficiently they often need to use bespoke hardware or software implementation, the installation, programming and maintenance of such systems as tasks that can only be carried out by specialists. There are a number of standard programming methodologies that are usually supported by Supercomputer manufacturers and languages such as C, Java and FORTRAN are usually available. Currently only 4 of the top 500 supercomputers have a vector architecture however.

There are two other issues with specialist Supercomputers apart from cost: scalability and obsolescence. Scaling supercomputers is possible, but usually with the chassis as the lowest level of granularity, meaning that you will usually need to purchase more CPU's in batches of 128 or 256. Furthermore, since the hardware is bespoke, it may not be possible to scale at all if it is

---

[11] Eigenmann, R (2001) Performance Evaluation and Benchmarking with Realistic applications. MIT Press.
[12] http://www.purdue.edu/taplist/

no longer supported by the manufacturer. The life of a Supercomputer is short and it is often the case that it is obsolete within 6 months of it being deployed (sometimes even before it has been deployed), particularly at a time when the commodity chip manufacturers are increasing clockspeed and cores faster than Moores law predicts. This is why the top500 list currently contains 354 systems built out of Intel commodity chips and 79 built out of AMD chips. Many of these are not dedicated supercomputers *per se,* but are built out of cluster or grid technology. This ratio of commodity to bespoke hardware is only likely to increase in the future.

Supercomputers are used in applications in which large data sets and calculations in which parallelism (and quite possibly communication between compute nodes) can increase efficiency. They are found in such diverse application areas as the automotive industry, data mining, finance, gaming, cryptography and geophysics. Of those that have declared their interest on the top 500 list, the most frequent application area is Finance with 20% of the Supercomputers, Clusters and Grids registered.

FPGA – a programmable hardware solution

A Field Programmable Gate array is a semiconductor device that is essentially a set (Array) of logic elements (Gates) and interconnects that are reconfigurable "in the field" (hence the name "Field Programmable"), both programmable by the customer and reconfigurable at run time. In other words it is a flexible, programmable chip. FPGA's are found in mobile phones, network interconnects and in the control system of Harrier jump jets and more recently are becoming common in HPC applications and systems. The Cray XD1, for example has the options of including arrays of FPGA's in its configuration. The reason for the adoption of FPGA's in HPC is that FPGA is inherently parallel because of the configuration of the logic elements. At a 500MHZ clock rate an FPGA can implement 100 single precision floating-point units in parallel, all of which can run in a single clock cycle. The flexibility of the FPGA allows the construction of FPU's with greater accuracy, but as always there is a trade-off and more precision comes at the cost if fewer units. A typical speed-up that you would expect from using an FPGA against a standard single core chip of around 2.5GHZ would be 50-100x. The limit of parallelism and accuracy for an FPGA is related to the size (and density) of the unit itself.

Despite their reconfigurability, FPGA's are notoriously hard to program. At the lowest level, their behaviour is defined in a Hardware Description Language (HDL) [13] which is then mapped into a Netlist, a description of the connections and elements in the design. This is then fitted to the architecture using proprietary tools from the FPGA vendor. This is a difficult and specialist process which contributes to the long lead time in system and software creation and deployment (up to 5x longer than the standard software lifecycle for languages such as C++ or Java). There have been recent developments in C like languages that are designed to raise the abstraction level away from HDL and reduce the programming time and the development of *systemC*, a set of libraries implemented in C++ which make it possible to simulate concurrent processes, has lead to commercial products and tool-kits from companies such as Cadence. An approach based on standard C is available from Mentor Graphics, and Celoxica provide a tool-kit based upon Handle-C, a subset of C, with C syntax for parallel programming on FPGA's developed originally at Oxford university. These tools reduce porting time but cannot create code as efficient as that which is hand crafted. Furthermore this typically reduces potential speed-up by up to a factor of 5.

---

[13] VHDL and Verilog are the two most popular

General Purpose Graphical Processing Units (GPGPU)

Graphics accelerator cards are common in pc's and laptops as ways of offloading specialised processing for the rendering of images on screen. Graphical processing is well suited to parallel processing and these cards are essentially built of large numbers massively parallel floating point oriented processors. Manufacturers of these technologies have seen the potential for use of these, essentially parallel high performance units in areas other than graphics processing and there have already been some successful examples of adding GPU's to machines in clusters to increase processing power, specifically in the Oil and Gas industry. It wont be long before we see x86 GPU hybrids near the top of the top500 list.

Processing images for the screen however, does not require as much precision as many HPC applications, so GPU's are exclusively single precision floating point units. While this may be acceptable in weather simulation and seismic discovery, HPC in finance in particular requires double precision and so GPU manufacturers increased precision on their route-map. NVIDIA have recently released a double precision version of their Tesla card specifically to address this market.

Programming GPU's is not straightforward however, and code written for multi-core does not directly translate. NVIDIA provide the CUDA a C++ like API for programming their 240 core GPU and ATI provide CTM ('Close to the Metal') an Assembly-language-like approach. There are also efforts from MindAlign and GPUTech to provide more general abstractions for programming GPU offerings cross vendor. Having a single way of programming different technologies is clearly useful, and may start to increase adoption of GPU's in general for HPC applications, but there is always a trade-off of performance against flexibility that must be considered. For highest performance, the native libraries and languages provided by the vendors will be preferable.

NVIDIA are currently pushing forward with Tesla, a GPU designed specifically for HPC which has 240 cores each of which can each run a number of threads and clocks an impressive 993 Gflops and has access to 4GB of dedicated memory. Memory bandwidth is 120GB/S and data can be streamed on to the Tesla board as fast as a PCI-X interface will allow, which makes this the limiting factor in the speed-up. If you can contain all data in the Tesla memory, then peak rates can be achieved. Tesla is SIMD-like, as it executes groups of threads (32 in current architecture) simultaneously although this is hidden from the programmer and it appears as a massive multithreaded environment with 30,000 concurrent threads. As long as the programming model can support rapid development paradigms, it is likely that Tesla racks will be a strong contender in the Supercomputer market.

ATI are not moving quite as fast as NVIDIA, but the folding@home project has already produced a driver to run on ATI GPU's and since AMD's purchase of ATI they have been working on building a complete stream processing solution, including software and hardware stacks, their vision for the future is a fusion of GPU and CPU, which has manifested itself as the Firestream 9250 released in June 2008. On this front, Intel are in the vanguard and their Larrabee project is designed to compete heavily in the GPU market. Larrabee will be a 16 (or more) x86 mini-core chip with a vector unit and a short pipeline. With each core running 4 threads this is a 64 way parallel x86 processor with vector processing capabilities. Larrabee is essentially a GPU which can be programmed using the X86 instruction set, meaning that cross compiling C and C++ should be a breeze, although exploiting the multiple mini-cores may still take some work. Larrabee is not set to be a separate chip, but rather will be part of the standard Intel X86 offerings (the CGPU), making GPU's as graphics processors, unnecessary. Larrabee is due for release sometime in 2009, and all eyes are on Intel to see if it will grow at the expense of NVIDIA and ATI.

SOFTWARE STACKS – FROM PARALLELISATION THROUGH MESSAGE PASSING TO GRID

Alongside developments in hardware, HPC has benefited from developments in software. The first attempts at addressing programming of parallel architectures were to make modifications to, or new versions of, the standard languages, C and Fortran. Parallel FORTRAN includes directives similar to vector processing directives and a set of primitives designed specifically for fast, parallel matrix and vector manipulation. Operating systems have always been able to run multiple processes simultaneously and the posix thread model provides a useful interface for programming multiple streams. In a multi CPU environment this threading model provides some degree of parallel execution and has been adopted in general as a generic programming model, particularly useful in graphical and event driven processing. Because of its wide spread applicability in a number of problem domains, the C threading model has been widely adopted as a paradigm for parallel processing, especially across multiple CPU, SMP, boxes.

However, threaded programming is not straightforward, particularly in cases where memory is shared in global or static variables and steps must be taken (via a mutex or synchronisation) to avoid multiple threads changing variables that are available to all threads before a one thread has finished with them. Introducing mutex's essentially introduces blocks and can make processing serial for a period of time. Threaded programming is neither simple nor particularly safe. With the increase of multi core boxes we might expect multithreading to be on the increase. However, there is an alternative that is more simple and that could take its place, particularly on the server-side and particularly in calculation intensive code – OpenMP.

OpenMP

OpenMP is an API standard for programming in an SMP environment. It consists of a set of compiler directives that can describe the parts of a program to parallelise and environment variables that at run-time, stipulate the number of threads to run it on. Developed at SGI in the mid 80's OpenMP is supported by Microsoft, Sun, IBM, Intel and other compiler vendors on many platforms including Windows and all Unix flavours.

Of course, despite (or perhaps because of) its simplicity OpenMP has drawbacks. In particular the scalability of OpenMP code is limited by the architecture of the box that the code is running. More specific problems include the requirement for a compiler that supports OpenMP, and the lack of reliable error handling. The following Open MP code sample computes the dot product of two vectors in parallel.

```
#include <omp.h>
#include<stdio.h>
#include<stdlib.h>
int main(){
/***********************************************/
/*define variables and initialise
*/
/***********************************************/
int i,n;
float a[100],b[100],sum;
n=100;
for (i=0;i<n,i++) a[i]=b[i]=i;
sum=0.0;
/***********************************************/
/*Now we want to compute
*sum=sum+(a[i]*b[i])
*and since each product is independent we can
*compute this in parallel with a running sum
*(hence the 'for reduction) part of the pragma
*/
/***********************************************/
#pragma omp parallel for reduction(+sum)
        for (i=0,i<n;i++)
        sum=sum+(a[i]*b[i]);
/***********************************************/

printf("dot: %d\f",sum)
}
```

MPI

MPI (Message Passing Interface) was the winner in a battle for supremacy with PVM (Parallel Virtual Machine) for the dominant cluster parallelisation paradigm in the 1990's. It won because of its clear scalability advantage, relative simplicity and because of the widespread adoption of MPI as the message passing approach to parallel computation by vendors. MPI offers a standard way to distribute work across a cluster of CPU's and provides mechanisms to share data between compute nodes at run-time, for tightly coupled parallel applications such as large scale simulations that use matrix solvers. CFD (Computational Fluid Dynamics) applications like weather simulations or aircraft design are good examples of applications where MPI is likely to be found, either on a supercomputer or cluster.

MPI is a standard defined by committee which consisted mainly of vendors but does not seem to have suffered too much as a result. It is in its second incarnation which seems to have stabilised and has given rise to a number of free and vendor implementations. It is designed for running one job that occupies as many CPU's as possible and so is a good solution for cluster computing. There are language bindings for C, C++ and Fortran however other popular languages found in industrial strength applications such as Java, LISP and Ruby are not well supported.

Pipelining

The pipeline programming paradigm is common in parallel programming where elements of loops can be implemented independently. This introduces a high degree of parallelism, and lends to execution as a "production line". When building an aeroplane, for example the wings and the tail can be built independently of the fuselage and then put together at the end. Of course, not everything finishes at the same time and so there may be time wasted waiting for components to complete. This is the programming paradigm typically found in devices such as FPGA's and is also suitable for GPGPU programming.

SOA

It is perhaps unusual to find a discussion about Service Oriented Architecture in a chapter about HPC. SOA is more about flexibility and scale than performance, however increasingly a service-based approach is being taken in the development of large-scale commodity HPC applications. This is particularly the case now as these applications have to integrate into pre-existing enterprise architectures.

Whole books have been written about Service, Oriented Architecture[14] and we cannot hope to do it justice in a short section. However for the purposes of clarifying a definition we can consider SOA to be a distributed computation paradigm with two key elements – services and interface contracts. Services reside in an infrastructure and communicate through a set of common interfaces. The services are, for all intents and purposes, fully encapsulated, i.e. black boxes. Programmers know their function and know how to invoke them, but do not know how the function is implemented. Users of the service also know how to communicate with it, invoke it and what to put in to it and what to expect to get out of it. This allows services to be physically and logically located in different domains and on different hardware, yet to act as a coherent whole. There are certain advantages with Service Oriented Architecture, as such loose coupling gives ultimate flexibility. This is sometimes at the cost of performance and in management overhead. SOA is central to the way in which grid has been implemented.

SDK's and common API's for accelerator programming

We have already alluded to the problems in porting code to specialist hardware, with FPGA's being the longest lead time and Larrabee or the AMD/ATI fusion offering being having the potential to be the shortest. It is an unfortunate fact that that in order to exploit parallelism, code will have to be re-written. The advantages of MPI and OpenMP is that they have defined standards and so once code has been ported it should be relatively simple to move it between MPI implementations on different Supercomputer (theoretically at least). GPU and FPGA programming are still in their infancy and each vendor is trying

---

[14] Josuttis, N. (2007). SOA in Practice: The Art of Distributed System Design. O'Reilley

hard to establish their language and toolkit, there is little incentive to offer open, cross architecture tools as this prevents vendor lock in (which vendors don't like!!). There are companies such as MindAlign and GPUTech who have produced cross architecture toolkits such that code written for the cell can be run on ATI or Nvidia cards but where these tools win by providing cross architecture solutions they loose in performance as they cannot exploit all of the specifics of the hardware. At this point it is difficult to choose between proprietary or generic. If you need a GPU now to run your HPC jobs, you should evaluate the tools and decide which will get you delivered faster with the degree of speedup you require. The interesting entry is Larabee and the HPC community is watching closely to see how straightforward the SDK is and which HPC libraries are supported out of the box.

CLUSTERING AND BEOWULF

Clustering is not new and in the 1990's was a common approach to providing resilience and fail over for production servers. However, the high cost of dedicated supercomputers and their short useful lifespan caused scientists with a requirement for a large amount of compute to look towards clustering in the large as a way of providing supercomputer-like capability out of commodity hardware. Beowulf was born in NASA as a dedicated cluster of Linux servers that was cheaper than the supercomputer alternative for running parallel code. The key features of Beowulf over other clusters is that Beowulf provides a dedicated homogeneous cluster, using free software and a UNIX like operating system, networked into a small LAN. The cluster usually consists of a master node, which will have a keyboard and monitor attached and a number of servers. For all intents and purposes a Beowulf cluster will appear as if it is a single computer. This is very different from other cluster types such as a COW (Cluster of Workstations). Parallelism is usually achieved through PVM or MPI and problem domains are usually scientific computing. These problems often requiring inter-node communication for their solution for which fast interconnects such as Infiniband [15] or Myrinet [16] may be employed.

The network topology for systems such as Infiniband and Myrinet tend to be either a simple bus topology or (for extreme HPC requirements) a mesh topology. Mesh topologies tend to provide lower latency between each of the hosts. Networking performance and transfer rates are therefore improved.

It is possible now to boot a set of machines from a live CD and they will form a Beowulf cluster. The OpenMosix [17] project takes this concept further by providing a single distributed operating system which runs across the cluster. In this case parallelism can be achieved through simple threading models as well as one of PVM or MPI. Clusters are usually dedicated to a single task and run one job at a time, they provide a scalable and extensible alternative to supercomputers around the same problem sets, and in fact currently 406 of the top 500 supercomputers are clusters.

Replicode is a recently emerged technology from Waratek [18] which in a parallel to RAID for disks creates a striped and resilient shared memory for parallel compute over a cluster. This Redundant Array of Independent Systems (RAIS) is an abstraction layer that can be incorporated in virtual machines environments (such as JVM or .Net) and implements and controls thread level parallelism over large clusters. This is a new

---

[15] http://www.infinibandta.org/home

[16] http://www.myri.com/myrinet/overview/

[17] http://openmosix.sourceforge.net/

[18] http://www.waratek.com/

paradigm for cluster computing that is simple to use and implement as it just uses a threading model.

Beowulf clusters, although seemingly cost effective, are difficult to configure and maintain. They have been designed with the aim of exploiting clusters of CPU's to complete calculations that would be prohibitive on a single CPU. However, they have not been designed with resilience and reliability in mind and as such are difficult to run in a production environment as the only HPC solution. This is where grid makes its play as an HPC, cluster management tool.

GRID AS AN HPC SOLUTION

Whereas with HPC you deploy a solution with a fixed number of nodes on dedicated hardware, grid computing brings the flexibility of using standard non-heterogeneous hardware and standard operating systems, in which nodes can be added on demand. A standard software layers is applied across this infrastructure to achieve this. Key to the whole grid proposition is that dedicated computing resources are not necessary, which leads to many grids being built by reusing existing hardware to produce a powerful unified computing resource. No special networking components are needed for grid and grid computing is not limited to the local LAN. It is not unusual for MAN and WAN boundaries to be crossed when building a grid resource.

Grid is not strictly High Performance Computing and we will cover grid in its own chapter, however, it deserves a mention here because of its ubiquitous use as a tool to manage large and small scale distributed compute clusters for *embarrassingly parallel* workloads. Grid is essentially used as a resource allocation and management tool forming scalable, resilient clusters of up to 1000's of commodity compute nodes. Grids are typically formed of collections of standard processors and exploit parallelism to give speed-up. It differs from other HPC technology in that it is explicitly not designed to facilitate inter-compute node communication, all communication is via the central management node. Advantages of grid in HPC are the ability to collect and harness heterogeneous, disparate resources and the relative simplicity of implementation of compute node services, both making it highly cost effective. This has made grid the HPC facility of choice for CERN, investment banks, hardware design companies and scientific research. In the next chapter we will explore grid concepts more fully.

SUMMARY

There are many technologies to choose from, with a variety of programming paradigms, degrees of speed-up and with different infrastructural challenges. These technologies all have their place and they all have a market and the choice of which is most appropriate for your applications and environment will depend on a number of factors. The table at the end of this chapter summarises the main features of each of these technologies.

Table 1-HPC technologies, benefits and tradeoffs

	Cost	Speed-up	Latency	Program difficulty	MIMD /SIMD	Paradigm	Power per flop	Tasks	Applications
Super-computer	H	In proportion to the number of CPU's	L	Medium	MIMD	Message passing/ shared memory	L-M	Dependant parallel; Independent parallel	Research, Life sciences, Engineering
Cluster	M	In proportion to the number of CPU's	H	Medium	MIMD	Message passing	M-H	Dependant parallel; Best for Independent parallel	Research, Life sciences, Engineering
GPGPU	L	High	L	Medium - Hard	SIMD	Threaded	H	Dependant parallel; Independent parallel	Oil and Gas, Finance
FPGA	L	High	L	Hard	MIMD	Pipeline	Very L	Dependant parallel; Independent parallel	Telecoms, control systems
Cell	M	Mid	L	Medium-Difficult	MIMD	Threaded	L	Dependant parallel; Independent parallel	Gaming
Grid	M	In proportion to the number of CPU's	H	Simple	MIMD	Service oriented/ message passing	M	Independent parallel	Finance, life sciences, chip design

Understanding Grid

IN SEARCH OF A DEFINITION OF GRID

The term grid seems to be ubiquitous in the distributed computing field, yet it is very hard to define and even harder to contain. There are blurred distinctions between the grid, utility and virtualisation spaces and overlaps are becoming even greater with the emergence of dynamically scalable, elastic resources that generally seem to be going under the name of cloud computing. As we will look at these concepts in later chapters our focus here is specifically on what might be termed *traditional* grid computing – a way of combining disparate resources together for the purpose of creating a single shared compute entity that is suitable for large scale calculations.

Grid is a natural evolution of cluster technology, and it emerged from the academic and open source community during the 1990's in response to a simple problem, - there just was not enough computational resource available in any one research institution to provide for the growing computational needs of these organisations. Supercomputers were expensive (they still are) and relatively inflexible (they still are) and cluster technology seemed to be the answer. A combination of early successes in pulling together networked workstations inside a single organisation in a Beowulf style configuration with the rapid growth of the internet and associated standardisation lead to the first applications that could truly be called grid – Distributed.net in

1997 and then SETI@Home_in 1999.

The SETI project is well known as it was designed to support the analysis of observational data in the search for intelligent life outside earth. Less well known was its primary aim to prove the viability or large scale shared distributed computing. Its success was in the use of volunteer computing, exploiting spare CPU cycles from internet users happy to donate their CPU time to the project. Eventually this ran on over 3 million computers, many of which were home users desktops to process data at 23 teraflops. To date, no evidence of extraterrestrial intelligent life has been found, but the SETI infrastructure has evolved into BOINC, which is a generic platform for large scale, shared, distributed computing. Distributed.net was designed specifically to exploit volunteer resources in the same way, but in this case to break the RSA 56 bit encryption algorithm and win the $10,000 prize available. It is now working on the 72 bit key.

The success of SETI and distributed.net opened up possibilities for a massive shared computing infrastructure which could be funded through volunteers and a simple donation model (you add your PC or data center to the infrastructure, and you can use the infrastructure). In order to achieve this vision there were (and still are) a number of technical and standards questions to be resolved and it was really Ian Foster from Argone national labs and Karl Kesselman from the University of Southern California who coined the term "grid" and began the standardisation effort that eventually lead to the OGSA (Open Grid Standards Association) and Globus, the first reference implementation. Foster and Kesselman[19] saw a future in which compute resource would be available in the same way as electricity is, you pay for what you use and no more, and when you want it, it is available.

---

[19] Foster, I and Kesselman C. (1999) The Grid. Blueprint for a new Computing Infrastructure

They likened the compute service to the electricity grid service. Hence the name.

This effort has spawned a number of research programs and a proliferation of grid solutions from vendors and research organisations. At last count there were over 30 systems available that were labelled grid. A notable example is the EGEE (Enabling Grids for E science) project which was put in place to ensure the data coming from the high energy physics experiments at CERN has been immensely successful in bringing together 40,000 computers in 40 sites to form a single shared computing infrastructure to support a major project.

In the research and academic communities where resource is scarce and problems are potentially huge, grid makes sense. In searching for a true definition of the grid, in relation to the original vision we can put forward a definition of grid as a collection of resources glued together by middleware that provides connections and services for shared use. The challenge for the grid is "flexible, secure, co-ordinated resource sharing amongst dynamic collections of individuals, institutions and resources[20], capitalising on the fundamentally heterogeneous possibilities offered, whilst at the same time addressing the question of Quality of Service (QoS). This is the question of whether it is possible to guarantee QoS at all in an heterogeneous, pervasive, dynamic grid environment; one in which virtual organisations[21] can join and leave, or provide various resources at their own whim and as their own business dictates.

The vision of a shared, ubiquitous resource pool works well in

---

[20] Foster, I and Kesselman C. (2004) Grid2. Wiley.

[21] Virtual organisations are separate entities that are able to join and leave a grid. They typically provide resources for sharing and use other VO's resources. They can be separate physical entities or separate departments within a single entity.

research and academia but it is clear that there are significant blocks to inter-enterprise sharing in business or even intra-enterprise sharing of resources. There is no advantage for a business that can afford its own resources to donate them to a pool in which the combined compute capability would enable smaller businesses, at lower cost, to compete with them. As a result the focus of vendor based enterprise grid systems has been on providing an internal service based infrastructure for parallel computing. In many cases this is little more than sophisticated cluster management software. It is these grids that will be the focus of our discussion.

THE CHARACTERISTICS OF GRID

Grid is not High Performance Computing. It is important to make this point strongly and at the very beginning of our discussion. Grid does enable HPC by virtue of the amount of compute resource it can make available for parallel computation but it is certainly not the best option if the primary aim is that the computation complete as fast as possible. In fact traditional HPC applications such as CFD[22] and Weather simulations are totally unsuited for the grid. We will look at application patterns suitable for grid computing in a later section.

Amdahl's law

Amdahl's law gives a theoretical to the amount of speed-up that can be achieved through parallelism. Simply it states that the

---

[22] Computational Fluid Dynamics – usually associated with mechanical and aeronautical engineering simulations. Essentially the solution of differential equations, which can be expressed as sets of simultaneous equations.

limit to the speed-up of a system is the slowest part. The slowest part will typically be serial (unparallelisable) and in the master-worker paradigm this is usually the task distribution and aggregation parts.

More formally:

If S is the serial part of the calculation and 1-S is the parallel part then the maximum speedup is achieved when using P processors is

$$1/(S+(1-S)/P)$$

So, what is grid if it is not High Performance Computing? The following outline the four main characteristics of grid:

High *Throughput* Computing. Grid is essentially a scheduling and resource allocation tool. It is extremely efficient in locating suitable, available resource and scheduling work to it. Grid schedulers have the capability of scheduling multiple jobs from multiple clients and making sure that jobs are scheduled as early as possible, according to their priorities and permissions.

Highly *Resilient* Computing. One key design principle of grid is the "at most once" submission semantic. This means that once a task has been submitted then it is guaranteed to complete. Grid has a number of mechanisms to ensure this even in the case that the grid is completely down for a period of time (as long as not all of the machines are physically damaged). Grid components and grid tasks can fail-over and re-start even across sites that are separated by a WAN.

Highly *Scalable* Computing. To some extent this characteristic does depend on the jobs and tasks being run on the grid and any external dependencies (such as databases), however, it is broadly the case that if your application, or application suites (a more likely scenario) can benefit from having more resources available, then grid makes this a simple matter. The application, without re-work, can be made available on sets of new resources almost immediately and can scale as far as Amdahl's law allows.

High *Utilisation* Computing. The importance of this is coming to the fore more and more, especially as contribution of technology to the carbon footprint of the world is being realised and quantified and it makes good business sense. Compute resources are typically being utilised at perhaps 20% due to the unavoidable practice of planning capacity for peak rather than average load and the proliferation of fully fat desktops that often act as little more than word processors. Grid can harness spare resource and allocate tasks to it efficiently, this means that there is a degree of levelling of activity and through a combination of grid technology and process engineering important jobs can complete without the need for quite as much physical hardware. Grid has been known to drive up utilisation to 70% in some organisations.

In addition, there are a number of more specific capabilities and design principles of the grid that ensure the four key characteristics above.

Prioritisation – Tasks can be run at different priorities. There are a number of prioritisation models which we discuss later.

Sharing and reservation – Grids can be combined with portions of resources shared across lines of businesses, regions and even if appropriate, entities.

Service oriented – Grid components are usually hosted on multiple distinct machines (virtual or physical) and so the only option for software architecture is distributed and loosely coupled with each component making itself available as a service with a well defined interface.

Job management – Grids require efficient operational capability and the job management components ensure that jobs are started and finished when required, are handled as efficiently as possible, are monitored and reported upon, and most of all complete.

Whereas with HPC you deploy a solution with a fixed number of nodes on dedicated hardware, grid computing brings the flexibility of using standard heterogeneous hardware and operating systems, in which nodes can be added on demand. A standard software layer is applied across this infrastructure to achieve this. Key to the whole grid proposition is that dedicated computing resources are not necessary, which leads to many grids being built by reusing existing hardware to produce a powerful unified computing resource.

A grid can be thought of as a general computing resource in which different nodes of the grid work, in parallel, on computational tasks that have been broken down by the grid management software and farmed out using the grid scheduler. Unlike traditional HPC solutions each node can be working on different computational algorithms and tasks which, after being farmed out, are brought back together to calculate the final result. We will explain this in more detail when we discuss components and roles below.

In summary, grid makes good business sense, it can improve TCO, guarantee and ensure the timely completion of business tasks and can grow relatively painlessly with your business demands. However, much of this depends on the way you use it and your expectations.

GRID ARCHITECTURE AND STANDARDS

It is important to make sure that we are all on the same page with respect to terminology and so in this section we will define a few terms and outline a basic reference architecture before moving on to discuss the technologies that make ubiquitous grid possible.

Components and roles

All grids are based on a master-worker paradigm, with a manager responsible for distributing workload to workers which carry out the work. Rather than think about grid components, it is perhaps easier to think about roles and responsibilities. These can be mapped to the various implementations.

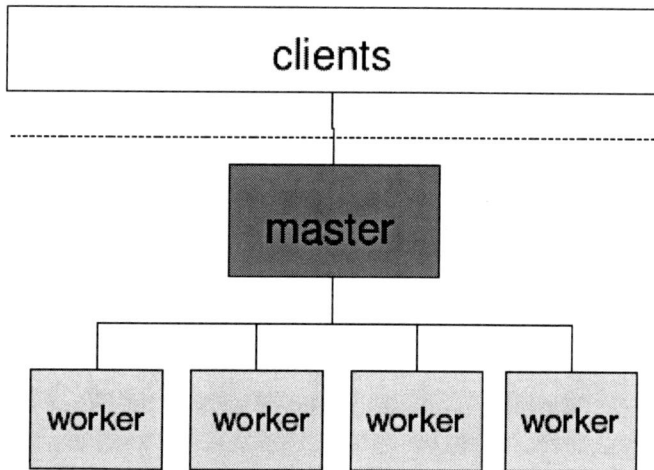

Figure 2 - Master Worker Pattern

The simplest component of the grid is at the worker end. Each compute node must be configured such that it can accept work that it is capable of performing. There are a number of ways of achieving this and solutions have been drawn from a body of knowledge about running remote procedures, code, components and services. We may think of the worker performing a service. Grid is inherently service oriented and it is appropriate to think of this worker services as a *black boxes* with a defined interfaces and outputs. The grid client does not need to know how the service performs its function, it merely needs to know the required inputs and outputs and trust the result (an interesting issues in itself).

Thus the worker needs to announce the available services and its status. For example, it would provide announcements about whether it is up and/or busy and also information about the quality of the resource (CPU, Memory etc.). The master has responsibility for resource allocation, for which it requires information from the worker, for job scheduling and prioritisation and for the management of users and groups. Manager components are also in control of resilience, fail-over and the centralisation of logging information. In implementations where multiple master nodes are needed to ensure line of business segregation or load balancing capability the master is often split by roles, with authentication and manager component resilience handled by a top level director and each grid cluster managed by a separate broker component.

Role	Component
Authentication	Manager/ Director
User management	Manager/Broker/Director
Resource allocation	Manager/Broker
Sharing policies	Manager/Broker
Deployment	Manager
Prioritisation	Manager/Broker
Worker management	Manager/Broker
Service provision	Worker

There are some grid technologies that do not include schedulers or job managers (such as GLOBUS), instead providing adapters for 3rd party components. This is a fair approach as it focuses on the truly core aspects of a grid (of which job scheduling is arguably not one). However most grid middle ware does include significant management components, and add a good deal of value by doing so.

Standards

The world of distributed computing, driven by the internet, Component Based Development and Service Oriented Architecture has moved to a loosely coupled architecture glued together with HTTP, SOAP, REST, WSDL and XML. Academic, research and Grid has wholeheartedly adopted these standards which has allowed the development of fully interoperable systems that allow sharing across organisations, regions and oceans. We give a quick definition of these standards in the table below, for more information take a look at some of the recommended additional reading. Third party, vendor systems may take advantage of some of these standardisations but pressure of getting to market quickly and the commercial advantages of proprietary formats has meant that as yet interoperability between any two of these systems is not possible.

For some applications the overhead of HTTP and SOAP are too much and direct socket connections are more appropriate. In the research and academic context job run times are typically in the order of minutes, hours or even days and researchers are more often than not glad that they have a large number of compute resources available that will shorten run-time from weeks to days and will not cost the earth. The grid middle ware systems developed under these constraints are suitable for batch processing but do not satisfy the needs of commercial organisations for interactive, intra-day, *as-quick-as-you-can-and-I-don't-care-how-much-it-costs*, processing. There are many terms to describe this, but we will call it *stream processing* to distinguish from batch. A significant requirement for fast submission of small jobs intra day is in the financial services world. Financial institutions are early adopters of grid technology and have shaped 3rd party products such that address stream and batch needs, this has caused a necessary drift away from standardisation.

To summarise how grid middleware works:

1. The scheduler spawns the tasks, loads the data and distributes them to the grid nodes

2. The workers on the grid node perform some sort of compute function on the tasks

3. A checkpoint status is done at some point during the work on each node in case a node fails

4. The data is brought back to a central location and aggregated to give a result

The main standards effort has not been in the technologies used, but rather in the definition of the services, roles and functions that a grid needs to support if it is to satisfy the requirements of the grid community for scalable, manageable, open, reliable systems that can build a reliable resource pool. These efforts have been driven by the Open Grid Forum (OGF) and has resulted in the Open Grid Services Architecture (OGSA)[23]. The OGSA has emerged from a seminal paper by Ian Foster[24] that describes a services based grid that assures interoperability between heterogeneous and widely distributed services resources.

The OGSA is both an architectural processes that seeks to maintain interoperability and openness in grid infrastructures through development of agnostic open standards and a set of specifications that document requirements for grid components. In particular it defines grid in terms of a set of capabilities:

❑ Infrastructure services

❑ Job management services

---

[23] http://www.ogf.org/documents/GDF.80.pdf

[24] Foster(1998). The Psychology of the Grid.

❑ Data services

❑ Resource management services

❑ Security services

❑ Management services

❑ Information services

The OGSA standards have given rise to the development of specifications for software components and, in particular, interfaces that describe the way in which the grid components interact. Initially this "plumbing" was defined by the OGSI (Open Grid Services Infrastructure) which has now been superseded by the WSRF (Web Services Resource Framework) which forms the basis of the specification reference implementation, GLOBUS Grid, which is commonly known as Globus Toolkit, and we are now on version 4 (4.2.1) (GT4). The Globus implementation through often criticised as being bloated is not really intended as a functioning grid, but as a reference for how it should and could be done. GT4 is functioning in the large and is also the basis of a number of other grid implementations, notably G-Lite that underpins the CERN grid.

Alongside the OGSA there have been attempts to standardise data access and OGSA-DAI has emerged as both a specification and implementation for sharing data resources in a standard way across grids. In order to simplify the process of grid on-boarding via standard API's have been proposed such as DRAMA and SAGA, but with not much success.

Of course the grid vendors have ignored most of these standards or, at best, paid lip service to them, in the interests of getting to market quickly and in pursuit of performance. In fact, interoperability between grid vendor systems would have been commercially problematic especially in an immature market. Now it seems, that this is much more of a possibility, although the jury is still very much out.

AVAILABLE GRID TECHNOLOGIES

Many have been heard to say things like "that's easy, I could write my own" and many have tried with varying degrees of success. Grid, after all, is just an extension of Distributed Computing mixed with aspirations of High Performance Computing and so it is building on a solid and well established foundation. With the libraries around today a Java, .NET or Python grid should take just a few days to get to the first cut.

Of course there is a lot more to it than just being able to fire up a few process on a few boxes and call them with some version of RPC. The real skill is in developing the scheduling, resource allocation, instrumentation and resilience capabilities and in making it a robust application. This can turn a few days into a number of man-years project. Nonetheless many have tried and some have succeeded in building grids that can be used for research, development and even production purposes.

Open source options

There is a mixed bag of free and open source options, not many of which are used in earnest in production. Open source grids typically adopt standards (but not always) quickly get to a critical mass through the use of standard components. However, they also have a habit, if not controlled, of becoming monolithic beasts which are hard to maintain, install and configure. This is not always the case.

It is worth bearing in mind as you look towards open source grids that you are looking to the community, or even yourself, to make functional changes and repair bugs. This is perfectly acceptable in some situations and not in others. You can decide. Many open source grids have not been tested in production or at scale and often performance is a question as the compromise between performance and openness swings, understandably, towards openness. In the following section we will briefly discuss some of the many open source or free grid solutions and their practical use.

ALCHEMI[25]

A free, open source, .NET enterprise grid solution that is easy to install and use. It was developed in Melbourne University and has an impressive list of case studies. There is no information about scalability or resilience/ reliability and the management and configuration tools are basic. However, it has been very successful as a university project and has a route map that includes Java and Linux integration. In its current form Alchemi is not a candidate for a high availability production system, but it is a strong contender amongst open source projects.

FURA[26]

Fura has emerged in response to Globus. The developers had worked on the Globus project and recognised early on how impractical it would be for the middleware to be part of a production system. They developed the GridSystems middleware which was open sourced in 2007 as FURA. FURA has minor successes with a number of Spanish companies adopting it as their grid middleware. Written in Java and using SOAP and HTTP for communication and transport it is a relatively open solution and includes some useful management and billing functionality. However, it is unclear how far it will scale and submission and transfer performance is an issue excluding it from stream processing.

---

[25] http://www.alchemi.net/
[26] http://fura.sourceforge.net/

GLOBUS[27]

It is hard to know what to expect from a reference implementation. It has every feature of the specification implemented, leaving it rather overweight for most tasks. The latest version GT4 is difficult to install and hard to manage and although it could be used to form the basis of a grid, it lacks a scheduler, although it can plug in Condor, LSF and many others. The focus of GT4 is sharing across virtual organisations and so certification and security form key elements of the implementation. It has been implemented in C and Java, and has a strong web services flavour. It is not suitable for short running jobs, or for jobs where a strict SLA is required. But it has formed the basis of a number of other grid implementations that have essentially stripped away unnecessary parts to improve management. Glite is the most successful and notable example of this.

Part of the Globus specification is GridFTP, which is an extension to the well-known file transfer protocol (FTP).

GridFTP extends the FTP standard with:

❑ Strong authentication, encryption via Globus GSI on both control (command) and data channels

❑ Multiple data channels for parallel transfers

❑ Third-party transfers: C can initiate a transfer from A to B

❑ Partial file transfers

❑ Reusable data channels

❑ Tunable network & I/O parameters

❑ Server side processing

---

[27] http://www.globus.org/toolkit/

❑ Command pipelining

GridFTP enabled servers are often used as a means to distribute data amongst shared file systems on varying grid implementation. UberFTP is the GridFTP server that is included with the OSG release.

GLITE

Glite is the middleware that drives the European Grid (EGEE), which has been developed primarily to support the analysis and processing of data emerging from the CERN high energy physics experiment[28]. The volumes of data processed and the size of the grid are an impressive achievement. It is planned that the European Grid will process 40TB of CERN data daily, over 40,000 compute cores in up to 40 locations. This grid infrastructure is available to any contributing academic institution for processing not related to the CERN project and Glite has been rolled out in unconnected clusters to support a number of research and development projects.

As a cut down version of Globus it suffers many of the same support and maintenance issues and is focussed very much on batch processing. Glite is unsuitable for very high availability, high performance clusters and is particularly unsuitable for stream processing. The maintenance overhead makes it a costly solution for a production system.

ICEGRID

ICE is a true middleware and along with an event driven message passing distributed compute infrastructure, deployment tools and performant mechanism for remote function invocation it has a certain amount of grid functionality. ICEGrid provides simple resource allocation capability that coupled with the depth

---

[28] https://lhc2008.web.cern.ch/LHC2008/

of the ICE stack can form the basis of a scalable, performant grid solution. However, it is only the framework and there will be some significant development necessary to integrate useful scheduling and resilience. ICE is licensed under GPL so beware of the licensing implications of building a grid solution with it, but it is a well-designed scalable performant middleware with a variety of language bindings that could certainly be a good basis for a bespoke high performance grid.

SUN GRID ENGINE

The Sun offering in the grid space has a long pedigree. The SGE and commercial product N1 grid are based upon the GridWare product, which they acquired in 2001. Essentially as a batch scheduler it has a lot of good features and it has become a very usable part of the sun stack. It has a number of users in finance, pharmaceuticals, academia and engineering but is not really suitable for interactive and short running jobs. Despite being a SUN product it is predominantly implemented in C but nonetheless comes with a number of useful configuration and management tools and is available across Windows and Unix platforms. SGE has a number of traditional grid features including a number of scheduling algorithms, policy based allocation and job check pointing. SGE is a credible free alternative to 3rd party grids for batch processing but is yet to be tested at scale or in multi-cluster environments.

Vendor solutions

There are a number of grid solutions available that you can pay for, and with so many free ones, you might be asking yourself why you would. These third party grids are in the main proven in production, proven at scale and proven in performance and they add value through being reliable, straightforward (usually) and supported. If this is what you are looking for then one of the following may be where you should look, initially at least.

DATASYNAPSE GRID SERVER[29]

DataSynapse Grid server is a mature grid middleware that initially arose in response to the needs of the investment banking community and is now growing out from that sector, albeit slowly. It is the predominant vendor in the finance sector and is cited as managing grids in excess of 20,000 compute nodes.

The architecture is Director, Broker(s), Engine(s) and communication is based around HTTP message passing. Predominantly written in Java with .NET and C++ bindings it comes with an Excel adapter, an integrated data cache (not recommended for use even by DataSynapse) and uses a novel way of passing data around by reference. It is proven in production, is reliable and has a good set of management and deployment tools. Supporting batch and stream jobs it would be a good selection for mixed workloads, high utilisation and large-scale grids.

DIGIPEDE[30]

A native .NET implementation of a grid that was once favoured by Microsoft, Digipede has not made the impact that it hoped. It supports only .NET and works well in a Windows only environment but there are no published details about the scale or performance characteristics. It is easy to install and simple management tools are available, interestingly the fail over component is an additional purchase. It is unclear how Digipede will fare now that Microsoft have their own .NET based compute cluster server.

---

[29] http://www.datasynapse.com
[30] http://www.digipede.net/

MICROSOFT COMPUTE CLUSTER[31]

Microsoft is offering is growing in capability and initially they did hire key resources from Platform computing to get them in the market. At the moment the compute cluster is little more than sophisticated cluster management tool with a scheduler, but Microsoft as always never do things by half, and are likely to end up with a competitive and well-integrated product. At the time of writing it supports clusters of up to 2000 compute nodes and gives access to all of the Windows performance management tools for instrumentation and clustering tools for fail over. There is promise that it will include better scheduling capability, full resilience and a data cache and it is certainly one to watch for in the future. If you need a smallish cluster and you are very Windows oriented, this may be a cheap option, although most of the other tools have a significant Windows offering.

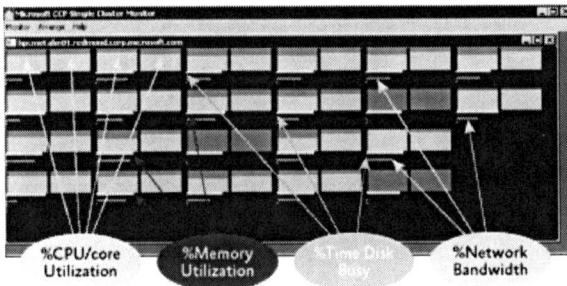

Figure 3 – Screenshot of CCS Simple Cluster Monitor monitoring several nodes.

PLATFORM LSF

LSF is another cluster or workload management tool with a long pedigree. At least 15 years old it started life as a distributed compilation tool and quickly became standard as a batch management tool for large clusters and supercomputers. It is not strictly a grid but is now available as a component of platform's

---

[31] http://www.microsoft.com/HPC/

other product, Symphony, and is based on Platform's Enterprise Grid Orchestrator (EGO). It is currently on Version 7 Update 3 at the time of writing and as befits such a mature product has a large install base (over 2,000 customers) and works in many heterogeneous environments.

There is available a Platform LSF -> Microsoft CCS bridge. The bridge was developed in a joint partnership between Microsoft and Platform Computing. The aim was to provide a more flexible and integrated solution incorporating both technologies. The integrated LSF-CCS solution enables the ability to allocate resources and schedule jobs in real time through a single management console, leveraging the performance and capacity of both cluster and data center environments.

PLATFORM SYMPHONY[32]

Symphony emerged out of the needs of the financial industry and in fact the initial release was developed with and jointly owned by JP Morgan. At the time (turn of the century) JPM were buying compute cycles from a Cray in a US University and were using LSF as the workload management tool. They found that although their batch needs were satisfied their interactive, stream needs were compromised by the latencies introduced by the location, scheduling and technology. They wanted to bring the compute solution back in house and so they struck up a partnership with platform to build a grid with the features they needed. Symphony emerged. It made a slow start in the finance industry and lost early ground to GridServer, although of course it drives the many thousand node JPM Compute Back Bone. Now disconnected from JPM, version 4.0 released 2008 it has many of the required features and competes in terms of performance and scalability. Written almost entirely in C++ Symphony has a multi manager architecture and boasts a proprietary transport protocol which

---

[32] http://www.platform.com

boosts performance. It remains to be seen if there is room for Symphony in an already stable market.

UNIVA UD[33]

Univa started life as a commercialisation of the Globus toolkit with the company providing support and maintenance contracts for users (many of whom came from the life sciences). A recent evolution of the company has seen a more targeted commercial focus and although they continue to support the open source community[34] (). Their new product Grid MP (v 5.6) is based upon web services and provides desktop harvesting at scale, although it is focussed still on batch jobs. A key differentiator of the technology is its support for MPI and it significantly improves over Globus in terms of installation and maintenance.

Any of these solutions will work, you need to pick the one that best matches your requirements. As you move towards selecting a grid you should run a proof of concept using your own application and thinking about the important criteria. These can all be easily tested, with perhaps the exception of scale – and which may create a large credit card bill on the Amazon Web Service. It is important to think of manageability and reporting alongside scale, resilience and performance as these are typically the significant differentiators from the open source offerings.

APPLE XGRID[35]

If you network your Mac you can Use Xgrid to distribute work effectively. Unlike grid solutions such as DataSynapse or Platform which sit on top of an OS Or VM technology, XGrid is a core part of the Mac OS. It does exactly what you would expect it

---

[33] http://www.univaud.com/hpc/
[34] The express version is available from http://grid.org
[35] http://www.univaud.com/hpc/

to do, it acts as a job scheduler allocating tasks to various nodes.

An XGrid job is submitted from the client to the controller, it is split into individual tasks which are sent for processing to individual agents on the XGrid cluster, these individual computers compute their portion of the tasks then return them to the controller which assembles the job then returns the results to the initiating client.

Essentially to work with XGrid, you need to run the XGrid Server admin application and select the XServe service. The XGrid admin has GUI support for them managing not only the grids, but also the agents and jobs.

Whether or not you could replace a 3rd party grid with Xgrid depends on your requirements. Certainly our investigation we quickly found limitations in terms of adding jobs, which has to be done via a terminal, although you the freeware GridStuffer provides a UI for this. Other useful add-on's are XGrid FUSE and GridEZ. Xgrid FUSE may be useful to you if you use Xgrid a lot and you are looking for something to check your job results without the command-line or some other GUI tool. GridEZ is a framework aimed at Cocoa developers that want to add XGrid functionality to their app. GridEZ works as a wrapper around XGridFoundation

XGrid seems to have been used in fairly specialized applications. Some products that support XGrid include Terragen, Blender and POV-Ray, all three of which are rendering tools. XGrid also has a (sort of) alternative to Jini in Bonjour which is a service discovery tool for finding services on the local network. It uses multicast DNS. You have probably used it without knowing if you have a Mac and you have installed and used ITunes (Bonjour is an optional set up on Windows).

XGrid is an interesting, powerful technology but inaccessible for most companies, which is a shame.

GIGASPACES XAP[36]

GigaSpaces XAP is not recognised as a traditional grid server product but it is more than capable of performing as such, with the added benefit that it has the DataGrid built in. Indeed one of the examples it ships with is a Monte Carlo Simulation. GigaSpaces XAP also integrates with DataSynapse and Platform computing.

One of the reasons it lends itself well to a grid server is that it is based on JavaSpaces, which implements the Master-Worker pattern. It has a sophisticated management console which enables real time service level agreements to be fulfilled, but it lacks the more sophisticated scheduling capabilities of some of the pure play grid server products. Despite its ability to be used as a grid solution GigaSpaces does not position its product as such but this is a valuable capability which you could used if your use case for grid needs access to a lot of data.

Product Summary

We have barely scratched the surface of the available grid middleware out there, and as we write we are sure that someone is building their own to add to the mix. In the end though they all do the same job – manage infrastructure – and there are some very simple principles for development and management which if applied can make the grid a solution rather than a problem. We will look at some of the grid best practices in the next sections.

PROCESSING DATA ON THE GRID - A NEW PARADIGM FOR GRID COMPUTING?

The success of search engines such as Google and Yahoo is

---

[36] http://www.univaud.com/hpc/

due to not only their capability to collect and store data relating to websites but also due to their capacity to process, filter and query data in a meaningful way. They do this using large farms of commodity hardware and using parallel data processing patterns. It is not exactly grid, but then again its not exactly HPC and the paradigms are more related to compute than data which is why it is included in this chapter. There are two initiatives that are useful to discuss here, and it is very likely that grid and data grid vendors will look at ways of implementing these patterns in the near future. In fact, some already have.

HADOOP AND PIG

Hadoop[37] is an open source Java software framework that supports the data intensive applications such as search and query. It can scale over thousands of nodes and can process and store Petabytes of data. There are two key parts of Hadoop, a distributed file system (HDFS) and a Map-Reduce engine. HDFS stores files over a number of machines (3 by default) and although efficient has some limitations particularly around resilience and time to recover after failure.

The Map-Reduce paradigm is not specific to Hadoop, in fact is was first put on the map by Google. It works on a master worker topology (like Grid) in which the master node decomposes the task into smaller sub tasks and distributes these to worker nodes, this is the Map stage. At the Reduce stage the master combines the outputs to generate the result. What is different here about this and the grid is that map-reduce allows the distributed processing of the map and the reduce operations. This means that independent tasks can be decomposed in parallel, and the aggregation steps (reduction phase) can take place on the grid as soon as results are available, making the process much more efficient and using the power of the grid or cluster to perform the

---

[37] http://hadoop.apache.org/

operations rather than putting load on the master node.

In Hadoop the JobTracker is responsible for workload management and it manages the Map and the Reduce tasks. This JobTracker performs similar functions to the Grid Manager. It has far fewer features than the standard Grid managers, is very simple in terms of scheduling, and currently has little or no resilience qualities. It is the unique combination of the HDFS and the map-reduce paradigm that makes Hadoop suitable for large scale data processing. In February 2008 Yahoo announced a 10,000 core Linux based Hadoop cluster.

The Pig[38] project started in 2007 with the aim of providing a simple, optimisable way of expressing data analysis programs. The idea was to combine knowledge of parallel databases, and distributed computing and to develop an abstraction that would be suitable for all paradigms. It currently provides a language (Pig Latin) and compiler that produces sequences of map-reduce programs. It has evolved as a sub project of the Hadoop project.

Pig is a significant addition to Hadoop, making the map-reduce paradigm simpler and more available for large scale distributed applications. Some data cache vendors are already implementing map-reduce in their offerings. If not Hadoop and Pig, but the concepts they embody are technologies to keep your eye on.

CHOOSING APPLICATIONS SUITABLE FOR GRID

Grid is not as complex as it seems, and there are a set of standard patterns and approaches for both developing applications for grid and for building out grids, small and large, in your infrastructure that can be learnt from and in many cases applied directly. This chapter outlines industry best practice in

---

[38] http://hadoop.apache.org/pig/

these two areas. Remember though that all generalisations are wrong, and that rules are meant to be broken, the key here is to apply best practice when it makes sense, and create new best practice when necessary. All of the patterns and approaches outlined in this chapter are taken from real-world case studies in a variety of industries, and typically will be found more than once. The experience that we draw on here is of developing for grid and for engineering grids in production environments.

The first and most important way that grid is used is in enabling job parallelism. A task is divided into subtasks and the subtasks are distributed and run in parallel. It is clear that not all applications are appropriate for grid. Certain classes of applications are easily parallelisable and simple to integrate and others can benefit from parallelisation but introduce management and development complications. There are applications that cannot be parallelised at all that may also be suitable for grid. The main points that need to be considered when deciding on suitability and porting effort are latency, sub task (or task) Run time, sub-task independence, state and whether or not the job is IO or compute bound.

LATENCY AND SUB-TASK RUNTIME

In this context we use the term latency to refer to the time that is added to the total job run time (turnaround time) by the grid itself. This is essentially the sum of the time from submitting the subtask to the time it arrives at the compute node and the time the subtask finishes and returns to the client, and it includes time queuing and scheduling as well as any network overhead, which is of course partially dependant on the size of data being distributed and the number of subtasks. You can also think of latency as the turnaround time minus the average subtask runtime, and it is usually measured in this way by repeatedly running a job consisting of one subtask and establishing the mean and standard deviation of the results.

If you were to discuss grid performance with a number of grid users there would be a variety of points of view of what was meant by the term high latency. For a local, dedicated or enterprise cluster for use in pricing financial instruments in the day then latencies over .5 seconds would be considered high, for a media company rendering images for the latest animated feature a latency of a few seconds would go unnoticed. Grid vendors strive to reduce the overhead of running on their grid, and this is a good thing in general, but latency cannot be considered in isolation from subtask run time when it comes to application and infrastructure design.

The key factor here is the ratio of the latency to the subtask runtime. Clearly for a job that consists of a single subtask, where the grid latency is greater than the subtask run time there is no sense in putting the job on the grid at all, as it will take at least twice as long as it would have if run locally. Generally you want the ratio:

$$(SubTaskRunTime/Latency) > 1$$

The higher the better. As a rule of thumb you want to aim at least for a value of 2 at which point you are adding only 50% to the job run time, which may be offset by the other benefits of the grid (such as resilience, throughput etc).

Rarely does a grid run a single subtask. Most applications running on a grid achieve speed-up through parallelism, and this has a simple effect on decisions about subtask run time.

Consider a job that takes 100 seconds and can be split in to any number of parallel subtasks. Splitting and merging takes .5 seconds. Grid latency is 0.5 second for a single tasks and has been seen to be constant for up to 100 tasks. Taking Amdahl's law into account we know that we cannot spread this job across an infinite number of grid nodes, because the grid latency will increase as the number of subtask dramatically increase but lets assume for the moment that it stays constant. If the job is split into 100 subtasks, the run-latency ratio will be 2, and the job will take a total time of 1.5 seconds plus the time taken to split and merge the job in the client, 2s.

Split this into 1000 subtasks and the job takes 0.1(runtime)+0.5(latency) +.5(splitting and merging)= 1.1s. Splitting into 10,000 tasks will give a job runtime of 1.01 seconds. Here we see that the minimum job run time can be expressed as:

Runtime + Latency + Lim $_{NumberOfSubtasks \to \infty}$ *(1/NumberOfSubtasks)*

At the other end of the spectrum, if we split this into 10 subtasks the total runtime is 11s. There are benefits from splitting, but the benefits become less the more you split. This is more evident if you also include the increase in overhead as the number of subtasks to schedule and overhead associated with the network traffic increases.

Independence

Grid has not been designed to run jobs that have subtasks that require interaction with other subtasks. The best type of job to run on the grid is one which is *"Embarrassingly Parallel"*. In this scenario each subtask is responsible only for its own state and its own completion, and it can fully utilise the resources that are allocated to it. On the other hand sub-tasks that require intermediate results from other sub-tasks will be blocked whilst waiting and will unnecessarily lock up grid resources. There are patterns in which it does make sense to have some sub tasks waiting to receive data from other sub-tasks, such as using an asynchronous writer (which will be discussed later on in this chapter) but in general inter-dependence should be avoided.

State

The question of state is a difficult one in the grid world. As a rule, Grid sub-tasks should be stateless. This simple idea is often very difficult to achieve as there are often efficiencies that can result from statefulness. One way of thinking about statefulness is that any sub-task which is linked to a physical location is stateful. If it matters which physical machine it runs on it is stateful. An example would be a sub-task which leaves residual data for a following sub-task, or requires data left by a previous sub-task. Constraining jobs in this way obviously creates issues for the scheduler and can have a significant effect on utilisaton and resource availability. Sometimes maintaining state in a job is unavoidable, particularly in multi-stage jobs in which the results from one set of sub-tasks are required for the next set.

State would typically be written to the local disk, may reside in local memory or could be written to a grid wide data cache or shared file system. In a number of grid configurations Databases serve as persistent stores, and then eventually as a bottleneck as he number of compute nodes increases. The best configuration if you must have statefulness really depends on the application, the size of the grid and the available technology. It is typically best to constrain the state on a node by node basis by writing it locally to memory and disk, as global state management requires a data caching or similar solution.

Even supposedly stateless tasks eventually hit the wall in terms of latency and scalability on the Grid. If you again look at how a compute grid works it becomes easier to pin down exactly where such bottlenecks may occur:

Function	State Impact?
Spawn tasks and load data	Yes – possible contention or database or file system.

Checkpoint Tasks	Yes – often done on a file system. Aim is to not to have to start node processing again on failure.
Store state	Yes – state may have to be stored when tasks are recursive, often the case with risk based tasks.
Aggregate Result	Yes – often done in a database (consider Map-Reduce paradigm).

The result of this is that we find that even for inherently stateless tasks we find adding more nodes and workers can actually result in the Compute Grid slowing down. When this occurs it becomes important to look at state bottlenecks and also other factors such as task sizes etc. If state becomes a factor then you should consider a DataGrid which we will discuss in further details in the DataGrid chapter.

Compute or I/O bound?

Grid has emerged from the HPC sector and is designed to solve problems that require lots of compute. Often these problems will require lots of data, but for a job to really benefit from the available compute it should be more focussed towards integer and floating point calculations than constant memory, network or disk access. The CPU is, after all, a computing resource. Too much I/O can have significant impact on sub task and hence job run time. There are high performance and scalable ways of delivering data, and there are simple ways of reducing I/O such as loading all required data at the start of the compute sub-task and writing results at the end rather than constantly reading and writing data during the sub-task run. Log files can be a significant overhead, so it is important to be aware of the granularity of your logging.

Fit-For-Grid?

The upshot of all of this is that grid jobs should really

❑ have a subtask/latency ratio > 2

❑ be stateless

❑ be embarrassingly parallel

❑ be compute, not I/O, bound

A general rule of thumb is that you should find another solution to solving your performance problems other than grid if the job doesn't fit match these categories.

The easiest issue to deal with is the subtask-latency ratio, this is managed by sizing the compute task so that it has a long enough run time. Statefulness can be dealt with and although it reduces your resource allocation options many commercial and open source grids have mechanisms for doing this. Jobs that are not embarrassingly parallel should never be put on the grid, there is no way round the problems that this will cause. The only exception to this rule is in the case of asynchronous data updates between nodes, in which the problem of blocking is eliminated. Grid is a compute solution and the single biggest problem in grid performance is caused by increased I/O, quite simply I/O bound jobs are not at all suitable for the grid.

Not all jobs that people want to put on the grid are like this. Sometimes the features and functionalities of the grid are sufficiently important for wholly unsuitable applications to be on-boarded. Later on in this chapter we look at some application patterns that help in designing architectures for jobs that do not fit neatly in this fit-for-grid category.

APPLICATION ONBOARDING

In this section we look at ways of on-boarding applications to the grid. We first of all consider the most basic and most prevalent pattern, and then look at ways of adapting this to meet other requirements. At the basic level programming for grid is no different to programming for SOA or any basic client-server system. The difficulty comes in understanding how to parallelise.

Parallelisation

Parallelisation can occur at two levels in the grid. In the first instance a single job can be split into independent subtasks, each subtask is then run and then the results aggregated. A good example of this would be a Monte Carlo simulation in which a large number of independent simulations can be split across parallel nodes. Not all jobs can be split in this way, as this only applies to jobs where some parts can be run in parallel.

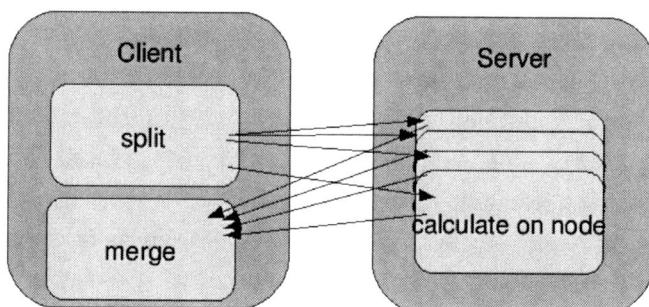

Figure 4 – Splitting and merging grid jobs

When individual jobs cannot usefully be split, then splitting can occur at the level of groups of jobs. For example pricing a financial portfolio requires pricing individual deals and then aggregating to the portfolio level. Each deal is priced on as a single job on a single node. Of course it is quite possible to split at both the portfolio and the job level, although there are some configuration considerations for multilevel submission, that we will discuss later.

Keyhole architecture

This architecture describes the basic way of getting a stateless, compute bound, embarrassingly parallel job on to the grid. It assumes that the job can be split into a client and a server part (see figure 5). This architecture is extremely flexible and allows independent enhancements to the service and the client as long as the simple interface is respected.

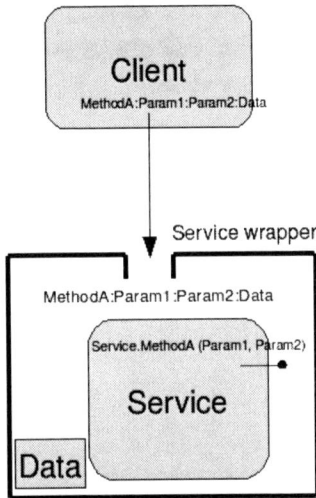

Figure 5 – Keyhole Architecture

The basic principle is to wrap the server side of the code into a service with a single entry point. The entry point expects a string to be passed from the client, and this string typically will include a service method name which is to be called on the service, the service parameters and any additional data required. The wrapper will understand how to parse this string and construct the correct method call. Passing a string avoids any issues with data type conversion and ensures that a client written in one language can call a service written in another.

The wrapper can be as simple or as complicated as required, and in some cases can load dynamic libraries and collect data from an alternative source before calling the method. The client will typically collect data and serialise it into a string alongside the method name and parameters for passing to the service. Of course, this string can be compressed for efficient passing across the network.

As an alternative to passing a string it is perfectly possible to use a web services architecture or for same language client and server scenarios using inbuilt object serialisation (which of course does the same thing, its just less effort). The key aspect to flexibility here in the keyhole architecture is to insist on a single entry point, similar to a RESTful architecture.

This simple architecture can for the basis of more complicated, more connected architectures and allows the gradual evolution of the service code without requiring client change, which is always useful especially where you have multiple clients – likely in the grid.

Writing data

The point has been made very strongly that I/O should be eliminated from grid sub-tasks if at all possible. However sometimes it is necessary to write results from grid subtasks to a data repository (Database or data cache). If at all possible these results should be written asynchronously and non-transactionally, as synchronous writing will be blocking. Best practice from distributed databases can be applied here, and if transactions are required then the method of *compensating transactions* should be applied. This is the approach in which data is written to the data store at all stages of the transaction, but in the case of a roll back a deletion message is sent. Of course there is a risk here that data that would be deleted will be used in the meantime, and if you want to avoid this then you must compromise by using blocking transactions, which are not good for your grid.

A common approach is to create a data-writer service that starts at the start of a grid job and is available to take messages with data to be written from each subtask. It will exist for the life of the job, and will be the only service with a connection to the data store (hence reducing the load on the data store). The grid sub-task will send the data to the data-writer service asynchronously by becoming a grid client and submitting its own data writing task via the broker, in which case it can benefit from the resilience that is built in to the grid. Should the datawriter service die, the grid will spawn another one and use that to write the data. It is obviously beneficial to have persistent data connection and the grid should have knowledge of any services that are alive and able to receive messages.

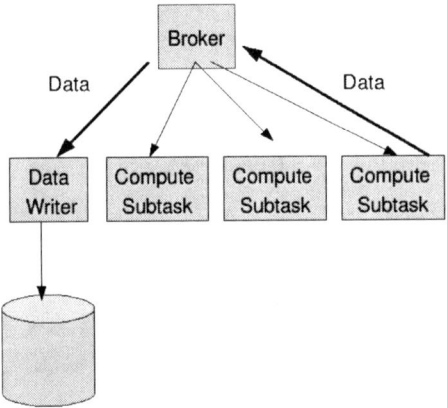

Figure 6 - Asynchronous Data Writer Pattern

Result Collection

There are three basic ways of collecting data from grid sub-tasks.

Immediate collection – a connection to the grid remains open and subtask results are send back to the client for processing as soon as they are complete

Deferred Collection – Jobs are submitted and then the client disconnects from the grid. Later on the client can lg in again and results from any completed subtasks will be returned to the client at that point.

No collection – The client disconnects and the results from the subtasks are written out from the subtasks to another system, queue, cache or data-store.

Deferred collection is a difficult paradigm as you can never be sure when the job is complete, and you must continually log in to check. This is equivalent to polling, which is essentially the way that immediate collection works. Furthermore with immediate collections errors can be handled when they arise rather than having to handle client re-submissions later. If no collection is a necessary pattern some additional, external job monitoring will be necessary. In general unless there are specific circumstances, immediate collection should be used.

Approaches to Concurrent Programming in Grid

As we have discussed Multi-core chips are now more and more predominant, especially in a distributed applications or a Grid environment where they very cost effective ways of generating massive amounts of compute.

Some HPC and Grid Platforms can take advantage of java multithreading and concurrent system and can take advantage of the increased processing power and utilise the CPU fully for more throughput. At a technical level Garbage Collection time, and pause time, is decreased using JVM garbage collectors (Parallel, concurrent mark sweep) that take advantage of more processing threads available in a multicore chip.

There are many new chips in the pipeline that will push the boundaries of compute power even further: Chips such as the AMD triple/quad core and the 8 Core on Bulldozer processor, the UltraSPARC T2 eight cores, with 64 concurrent threads. In the future we can expect to see these boundaries pushed even further. Intel has developed an 80-core processor prototype that has each core running at 3.16GHz, which it says will be released within the next five years. And of course there is Larrabee, a processor with many cores that is compatible with the x86 instruction set and capable of performing 1 trillion floating-point operations per second, it is no slouch itself !

Grid applications have typically been created as many independent parallel subtasks running a single thread per core. But with so much CPU available on a single machine it is time to look at this again. There are clear benefits from only scheduling sub task job that can exploit multi-core on a single CPU rather than having the scheduler submit each of the potential threaded tasks as a separate subtask. The advantage of a grid (that it is stateless and virtual) doesn't help here as data and tasks could end up on physically separate machines. There are certain advantages for certain applications for good locality of reference and multicore with multi-threading supports this. More so when the number of cores increases.

If we adopt this paradigm, essentially one multithreaded task per CPU (not core) we then have to enable Grid applications to take advantage of the multiple cores at the code level. There are a number of emerging concurrent programming languages that can help in this. Concurrent programming languages are programming languages that use language constructs for concurrency. These constructs may involve multi-threading, support for distributed computing, message passing, shared resources (including shared memory) or futures (known also as promises).[39]

Erlang is the most widely used general-purpose concurrent programming language. It was designed by Ericsson to support distributed, fault-tolerant, soft-real-time, non-stop applications. It supports hot swapping so code can be changed without stopping a system. Erlang was released as open source in 1998

Microsoft, has done some interesting work in this area with ideas borrowed from functional programming languages. The F# language is a direct result of this work. Microsoft make s the full source of the F# language available. Microsoft is aiming F# at Grid computing, and quantitative finance/banking firms consuming large grid resources

Maestro is another relatively new managed .NET-based Domain Specific Language for concurrent programming. Maestro incorporates well-entrenched language patterns and language constructs in a way to make concurrent composition more accessible and familiar to sequential code composers.

In all there are many concurrent programming languages that can be used for Grid and HPC, including concurrent C. However one has to take into account the cost, risk, and time required to move a sequential application to a concurrent one.

---

[39] http://en.wikipedia.org/wiki/Concurrent_computing

SOME TIPS ON GRID MANAGEMENT AND CONFIGURATION

Developing applications for grid is not independent of the configuration of the grid. The problem is that grids are rarely used only for one service or one application and so it is almost impossible to have the optimal configuration and arrangement for each job, and in fact there is usually a lowest common denominator configuration that on balance works for most jobs. Fortunately most grid middleware also allow you to set some parameters at a job or service level. In this section we look at some of the options for ways in which the grid can be configured to solve some key problems.

Synchronous or asynchronous?

Asynchronous job submission allows for jobs to be submitted in parallel, which means that the grid can schedule efficiently. Results can be handled as they return reducing the overall runtime of the job. There is no question that it is best practice to use asynchronous submission.

Multilayer submission

There may be times in which it the only possible approach is to write grid jobs that are themselves clients of grid jobs. In general this would be considered bad practice, since the grid job would need to keep alive waiting for its own subtasks, and therefore would occupy and block grid nodes. This could be particularly bad if the first layer of jobs already used 100% of the available resources. This is something to be very careful of. Using a collection method other than Immediate would help this situation, but does come with its own problems (see section above). As a rule of thumb, try and find another way of solving your problem.

If you must do it, then there are a couple of simple approaches to grid configuration that will avoid blocking. The first is simply to create two grids, or a hard grid partition and to allow the first layer of jobs only to be submitted to one of the grids. This still ties up the first grid, but you can use grid configuration parameters to ensure that there is good utilisation out of the remaining grid nodes.

The second approach is to configure more grid clients on your grid than there are CPU's and then to create a soft partition which includes these over-provisioned nodes only. This means that when a subtask submits back to the grid, and is blocked waiting (hence it is not using any CPU time) then the CPU can be used by one of the spare engines from the soft partition. This ensures that the jobs can complete and that the utilisation of the grid is high.

Resilient grid configuration

Grids are by their nature resilient, in fact the "at most once" semantic ensures that in order for middleware to be called a grid it must be resilient. Grid manager components have responsibility for managing the compute engines and ensuring resilience. A basic two cluster grid configuration is shown in the figure below[40]. Broker A and Broker B have sharing set up which allows either broker to allocate work to a proportion of free engines from a pool. Proportions of the engines would be homed to each broker but would for all intents and purposes form a shared pool. In the event of a failure of one or other of the brokers, engines would re-home to the failover broker.

Disaster recovery can be configured in a similar way. In traditional IT departments, It is usual for complete environments

---

[40] The term Broker is used here to distinguish responsibility for failover from other grid manager functions. A number of grid products make this distinction either conceptually or physically.

to be available for disaster recovery, but this is not practical with a grid as it could lead to having a thousands of compute engines available in a DR data center with a utilisation of close to 0. This would be costly, and so it is usual to create an active-active configuration in which a full production grid would be split across two geographically separate sites. In the event of power failure on one site, 50% of the grid would be available. If three sites are available then there is a high chance that 66% of a grid could be available in the event of a failure.

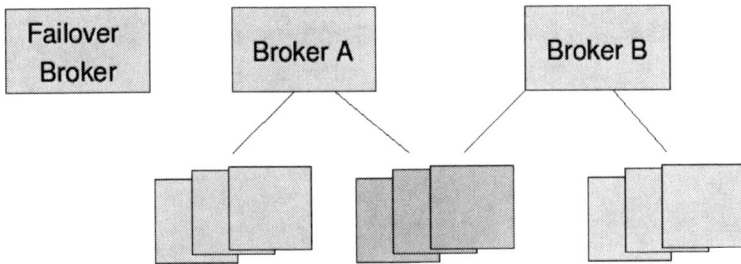

Figure 7 - Resilient Grid Configuration

SUMMARY

HPC and Grid Computing is prevalent in many sectors but up until now have been particularly successful in industries where large scale distributed compute is a requirement, such as in the financial, telecommunications and, engineering and manufacturing industries.

HPC and Grid technologies are fully integrated into the Financial Services having become an indispensable resource to both create market edge and to maintain competitiveness. Grid in particular is core to Option and portfolio pricing and risking and risk management in general. Before the use of Grid technology this would be performed overnight using batch processes but near real time calculation is possible.

Grid computing has also made significant inroads in the Telecommunications sector. It is helping carriers reduce costs, speed up their time-to-market, and extend their advantage over the competition. Unsurprisingly Grid has been used as a means to reduce costs by better utilising resources

Grid technologies can also offer significant competitive advantage and enable predictability around some uncertainties of scaling. For example, in the UK a major Telecommunications vendor used a Grid product to launch one of the most significant Smartphone launches in 2007 to ensure that their activation platform could handle large spikes and could easily scale.

Distributed Data Caching and Data Grid

This chapter covers Distributed Caching and also Data Grid. It begins with an overview of caching before looking at Data Grid product vendors, and what to look for when selecting a vendor.

WHAT IS CACHING?[41]

> *"A cache is a collection of data duplicating original values stored elsewhere or computed earlier, where the original data is expensive to fetch (owing to longer access time) or to compute, compared to the cost of reading the cache. In other words, a cache is a temporary storage area where frequently accessed data can be stored for rapid access. Once the data is stored in the cache, future use can be made by accessing the cached copy rather than re-fetching or re-computing the original data, so that the average access time is shorter".[42]*

The concept of caching has been well understood for a number of years and has been extensively utilized in the Von Neumann Architecture[43] but has only been fairly recently used to improve enterprise distributed architectures, and then often only in the case where such architectures have high throughput and suffer performance and contention problems.

---

[41] The word 'cache' is a French word meaning 'to hide'.

[42] http://en.wikipedia.org/wiki/Cache

[43] http://en.wikipedia.org/wiki/Von_Neumann_architecture

We can think of caching as a framework for data and state management where cached data is stored in computer memory.

There are a number of things to think of when considering caching. It is important first of all to understand why caching is needed in the first place. For example it could be for performance through data locality or to •prevent deep processing of data to reduce cost per transaction. It is also key that you understand the scope of the state you are caching. There are four states to consider

❑ Permanent state: holds the persistent application data

❑ Session state: Transient and exists only for a session

❑ Process state: Transient and only exists for as long as the process exists

❑ Message state: Transient and only exists whilst processing messages

The integrity of the cache must be thought about in any architecture. If the cache is a snapshot then you need to know when it becomes stale and how to ensure it is kept up to date. For example if the cache is fronting a database •and the database is updated from another external system then the cache could potentially hold "old" or "invalid" data.

Both the logical and physical scope of the cache should be addressed. In particular you should be interested in the physical and logical locations that it is accessible from. It is important to question whether the data being cached in the correct place. It could be at the session, SOA or Database layer, or in fact in another part of the architecture. This relates to the aim of the •cache, and is also important to know where else caches exist in the •architecture to avoid contention issues.

Cache can be resident in memory or disk, and the type of cache will have an impact on the architecture and on the performance and scale characteristics of the application. Access to data can be optimistic (assuming no transactions are in progress) or pessimistic. Optimistic locking is better for performance, but has compromises in terms of data integrity.

A cache is only as good as the quality of its data and Caches need populating and flushing. Data gets stale or expires. There are a number of security considerations around data that also apply to cached data, specifically around data access and trust boundaries and jurisdictions.

Finally caches need management, and the tools provided by various vendors are of varying quality. A cache will become part of your enterprise architecture and attention needs to be paid to how well it will integrate.

WHAT IS A DATA GRID ?

DataGrid or in-memory DataGrid is a relatively new term, and is used in a number of ways to describe a variety of tools and behaviors'. We can again turn to Wikipedia[44] for a good baseline definition

> *"A data grid is a grid computing system that deals with data — the controlled sharing and management of large amounts of distributed data. These are often, but not always, combined with computational grid computing systems."*

This definition is perhaps to "blue sky", so lets look at how the vendors of such products describe the term. Cameron Purdy, the founder of Tangasol, and the Coherence product, which was later sold to Oracle, provides the following definition:

> *"A Data Grid is a system composed of multiple servers that work together to manage information and*

---

[44] http://en.wikipedia.org/wiki/Data_grid

related operations – such as computations – in a distributed environment."

"An In-Memory Data Grid is a Data Grid that stores the information in memory in order to achieve very high performance, and uses redundancy – by keeping copies of that information synchronized across multiple servers – in order to ensure the resiliency of the system and the availability of the data in the event of server failure."

Nati Shalom, CTO of GigaSpaces, expands on these definitions:

"An In-Memory Data-Grid (IMDG) stores data in the memory of numerous physical machines instead of, or alongside, a database. IMDG is a well-known alternative to managing state data in a database— and perhaps the only one which releases the scalability bottleneck. It does this in two ways:

- *Eliminating I/O, network and CPU load incurred by opening database sessions, often to a remote database, and by writing data to disk.*

- *Partitioning the data and moving it closer to the application, eliminating the central point of contention."*

"In-memory data grids (IMDG) provide object-based database capabilities in memory, and support core database functionality, such as advanced indexing and querying, transactional semantics and locking. IMDGs also abstract data topology from application code."[45]

Pulling these definitions together we propose the following definition of an IMDG:

An IMDG overlays, integrates with, or works alongside a compute grid. Data is stored in memory

---

[45] http://natishalom.typepad.com/nati_shaloms_blog/2008/03/scaling-out-mys.html

so that it is more quickly accessible from compute grid tasks.

As compute grids have become more widespread in use, and uses of compute grids have become more complex, the need for a robust data infrastructure to provide fast and reliable data access and distribution is essential. Traditional compute grid product ship or work with either file systems. Messaging queues, or RDBM's[46], which become a bottleneck and a resource contention point.

WHAT PROBLEMS DOES A DATA GRID SOLVE?

No one in the commercial world uses technology for technologies sake, and there has been a reasonable adoption of Data Grid technology in a variety of sectors. This is because the features of Data grid help to solve issues that arise in data management and distribution in enterprise architectures.

Latency: Compute Grids are typically used to speed up batch processing operations that can take hours or days to complete. This has led not only to data being available immediately but to new business and revenue models, such as pricing of real-time risk on Capital Markets. Compute grids that spend a lot of time waiting for data that is required for computations mean that the service or tasks are not being run as effectively or as fast as they can. As mentioned previously this is normally due to disk-bound data access from file-systems or RDBM's. Time, as they say, is money, and one second saved can be millions of dollars earned particularly in the financial services industry.

Scale: It is often assumed that a compute grid process is stateless because a minimal amount of data is used against a vast amount scheduled tasks that execute in parallel before the results are aggregated. However:

---

[46] Relational DataBase Management Systems

❑ Data needs to be pre loaded for tasks

❑ Each compute grid task save state at some point in case it fails and so that it does not have to start from the beginning so slowing down the time to complete

❑ As tasks become more recursive state from one task may need to be saved and used for another task

❑ End results are aggregated often to a RDBMS

These state contention points result in Amdahl's law applying to compute grid's, and can lead to extra nodes being added, and the end-to-end latency increasing rather than decreasing.

Multi-tenancy: A Grid/IMDG infrastructure may be used by many departments for many different applications or services, particularly if the Grid is used within a utility compute model. For example, if one application requires replication between several IMDG instances, and another application needs to partition its data between the instances, the IMDG must be able to do both at the same time.

Data Affinity: Solving data affinity issues means that the data and the task are at the same place at the same time so execution can occur. That is the easy part. Doing it dynamically and on demand is the hard part. All the commercial vendors reviewed later purport to do this in one way or another.

Quality of Service (QoS): If a service fails on a grid node fails, it can result in loss of data. This could cause other grid operations to fail and subsequently cause not only downtime but also reliability issues. Ensuring the data is highly available results in much greater quality of service.

CACHING TOPOLOGIES AND PATTERNS

There are a number of ways of building and configuring caches depending on requirements. IT always comes down to a compromise between speed/latency and resilience and the following topologies demonstrate caching patterns at both ends of this spectrum.

Embedded Local Cache

An embedded local cache is the simplest of the topologies and is essentially a simple hash map for caching local data to work with local processes in non-distributed environments. Open source caching is often considered for these types of topologies.

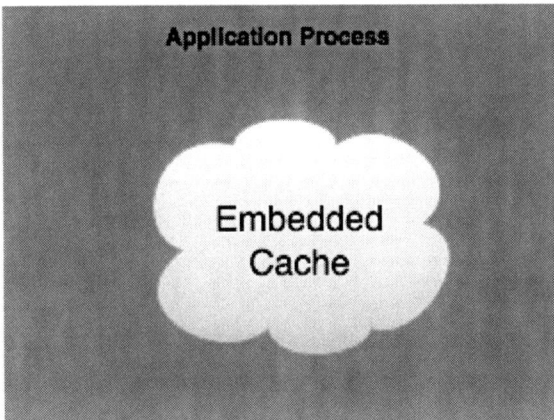

Figure 8- Embedded Cache

Master / Local Cache

This type of topology is also referred to as Far / Near Cache or Hierarchical cache (Gemstone) or Client / Server. This is a federate approach to caching data. Specific cache servers are deployed with the main cache and local cache's or far cache's function with the master cache in a parent-child type of relationship.

Master / local caching topologies can work with large client volumes and is often used in compute grid topologies in which the Grid Schedulers are integrated with the cache vendors so that data affinity and task affinity is co-coordinated.

- **Master / Local**

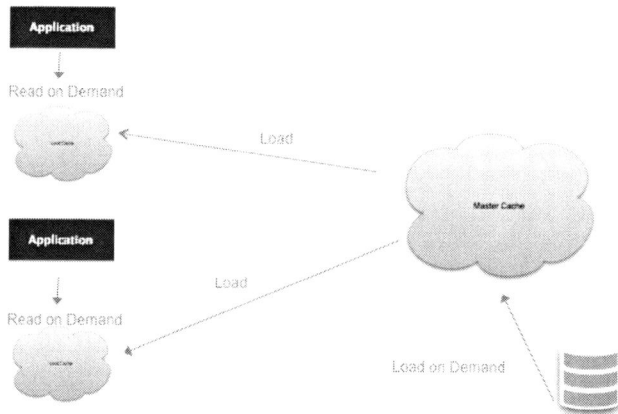

Figure 9- Master Local Cache

Replicated Cache

This topology is also know as peer-to-peer cache, in that there is no server application. In this cache con•guration, the cache is maintained locally in each peer application and shares the cache space with the application memory so execution is quick. All cache's are full synchronized. Write performance in this topology is quick. Note that Replication can be either synchronous (blocking) or asynchronous (non-blocking).

Cache instanced are synchronized asynchronously – Write performance to cache is fast. A Read can be done from any cache but updates can be done in only one cache so this topology provides scalable updates with locking

- **Replicated Cache**

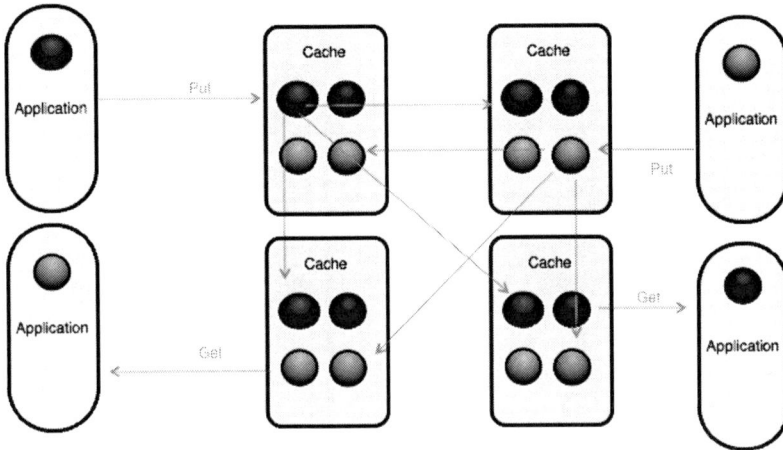

Figure 10 – Replicated Cache

This topology's primary drawback is its memory usage: because data is replicated to all processes, as data volumes increase, more and more data must be stored at each process. Also be aware that for scaling reliably multicast should be used.

Partitioned Cache

Partitioning can provide tremendous benefits by improving manageability, performance, and availability. It enables large datasets to be broken down on multiple nodes, which each hold part of the data, and map/reduce like queries to be conducted at great speeds.

■ **Partitioned Cache**

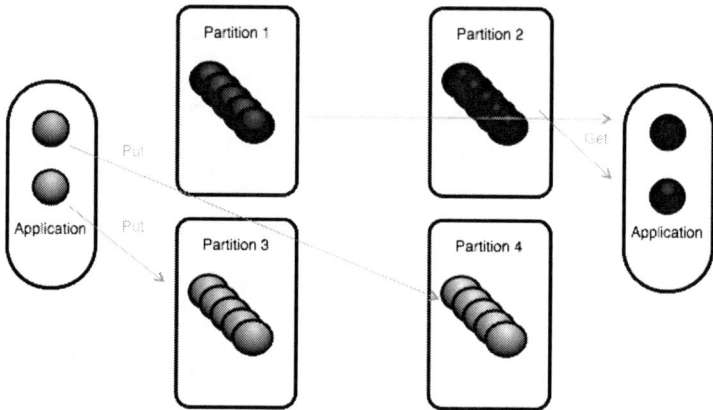

Figure 11- Partitioned Cache

Both read and write operations achieve better scaling using this approach and it means that data can be broken down and stored on many nodes. This is often called the "share nothing" architecture. One important point for partitioning is that it is essential to be able to identify a unique key for data for a partitioned cache to function.

Write through Cache

A write through cache writes data to the cache rather than directly to the underlying data store. Write performance is not improved with this method if there is synchronous write to the data store as the entry will not be marked as completed until it is entered in the data store. However, write performance is improved if there is an asynchronous write to the underlying data store

- **Write Through Cache**

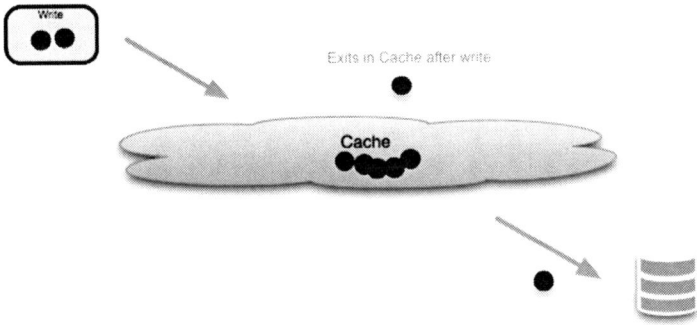

Figure 12 – Write Through Cache

Vendors have different methods as to how they handle this. For example Coherence uses something called 'Write-Behind Cache' functionality, whereas GigaSpaces can implement persistency as a service (PAAS).

Read Through Cache

A read through cache tries to read from the cache and if the data is not there then it is loaded from the Database into the cache. Write performance is not improved with this method. However, if a subsequent read operation needs that same data, read performance is improved, because the data are already in the in-memory cache.

- Read Through Cache

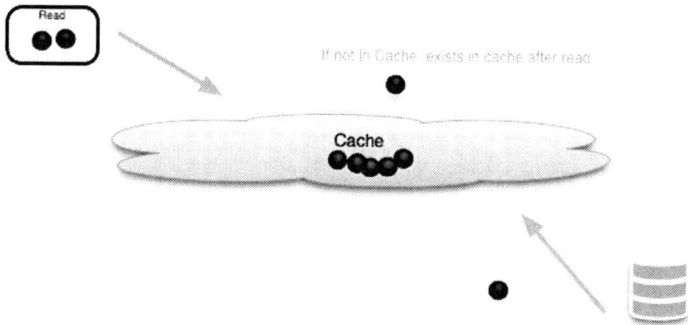

Figure 13 – Read Through Cache

OVERVIEW OF THE MAIN DISTRIBUTED CACHING AND DATA GRID VENDORS

Each of the main vendors provides a comprehensive product so a full in depth review of each could take up several books, we will spend just a little time describing each product and their main features. All are capable of functioning as DataGrids and IMDG's and each has various nuances and features that can help you differentiate.

GIGASPACES XAP

This product is an evolution of JavaSpaces distributed object technology and Jini Services technology. Both are still at the heart of the product.

The Core API is java, based on POJO and Spring. Other API's include .Net, C++, JDBC, JMS, MAP, Excel, and Scripting languages.

GigaSpaces XAP is multifunctional and can function as Compute

Grid and a DataGrid within one product offering. It has been Optimised form version 6.6 onwards for Cloud deployments and is unique in its SLA, provisioning, monitoring and management tools based on Sun's Rio initiative

GigaSpaces promote Space Based Architecture in which logic, data, and messaging tiers run from one container and everything's I virtualized to ensure lowest possible latency, greatest performance and easy scale-out.

GigaSpaces forms the core technology for low latency, scalable applications with distributed compute and data requirements in a number of sectors.

ORACLE COHERENCE
Coherence was originally based on a Jcache implementation and it had early success as bolt onto J2EE before moving into IMDG space.

The Core API is java, based on distributed Hashmap. Also supports .Net, C++ and JMS, and has successful implementation using Excel. Coherence has been successfully rolled out in production at the back of compute grids and as the basis of low latency applications.

GEMSTONE - GEMFIRE

Gemstone had been known for it's Object Database technology since 1982 and it was a natural evolution into in-memory distributed database. At the time of writing there are two product versions one in Java and C++. In fact the native C++ is big selling point and Gemfire also supports Java, .Net and JDBC.

Gemstone promotes their product as an Enterprise Data Fabric, and it is known to be focused at large scale, WAN level replication. It has been successfully integrated with large scale compute grids in major investment banks.

All vendors partner with DataSynapse and all vendors either

partner directly with or have at some point done some implementation work with Platform Computing.

APPISTRY

Appistry's Enterprise Application Fabric (EAF) is a platform for high-volume data and transaction processing. Appistry EAF is deployed across multiple computers in grid implementations. EAF has a feature called Affinity that helps to find data and run it on the associated machine. This improves overall system performance. Like more conventional DataGrid, EAF can also partition data within an application fabric and cache dynamic data for quicker access.

Appistry EAF can be used to develop task based applications with a strong bias towards workflow. From a caching perspective, it does have a built in caching component which it used for inter task communication, EAF also has strong multi language support (.Net, C and Java) and seems to have been used quite a lot for .net related Application projects. Appistry C++ interface is based upon buffers as opposed to function calls and as such lend itself well to the MPI pattern. MPI is extensively in academic area and in High Performance Computing as it supports Infiniband. One of it's biggest advantages is that it has built-in scatter-gather support.

A DEVELOPERS VIEW OF THE IMDG VENDORS

In this section we compare code for the three major vendors to show just how easy is to instantiate a cache and read and write an object to and from it. The object is specified below:

```
//The class to cache
public class Data implements Serialisable

      private long id;
      private String data;
      /**
      * Constructs a new data object
      **/

      public Data() {

       }

      Public Data(long id, String data){
            this.id=id;
            this.data=data;
      }
… getters and setters
```

The vendor code to create a cache entry for each of the three vendor products was implemented.

Gemfire

```
// Connect to the Gemfire distributed systems

Properties props = new Properties();
props.setProperty("name","Data");
.... set other properties
DistributedSystems ds =
SistributedSystem.connect(props);
      // create cache
Cache cache=CacheFactory.create(ds);

// Get the Data region,
// which is a subregion of /root

Region
dataRegion=cache.getRegion("/root/Data");

// write the data
Data data=new Data(new Long(1L), "some data");
dataRegion.put(data.getId(),data);
```

```
//read the data
Data data=(Data) dataRegion.get(new Long(1));
```

Coherence

```
// get the cache
NamedCache cache =
CacheFactory.getCache("DataCache");

// write to the cache
Data data = new Data(new long(1L),"some data");
cache.put(data,getId(),data);

// read from the cache
Data data = (Data)cache.get(new Long(1L);
```

Gigaspaces

```
IJSpace space = (IJSpace) new
UrlSpaceConfigurer("jini://*/*/space").space();
GigaSpace gigaSpace = new
GigaSpaceConfigurer(space).gigaSpace();

// just a simple pojo
Data data =new Data(new Long(1L), "some data");

//write
gigaspace.write(data);

//read using a template, can query on an
attribute
Data template = new Data();
template.setID(1L);
gigaspace.read(template);
```

Not surprisingly, all three implementations are very similar. In fact, in general they have very similar attributes:

❑ They are all easy to use

❑ Creation of a cache is very simple

❑ Writing and reading from a cache is straightforward

❏ All three provide in-memory implementations

❏ All of the implementations provide ways to add indexing for fast reads

❏ All of them provide mechanisms for advanced querying

❏ They support either SQL directly or have an SQL-like capability

❏ All of the them provide ability to add listeners on cache data change

❏ All of them provide transactions

❏ All of them provide locking

When considering a product from a commercial vendor it is important to look at a very broad set of features for current and future use. We consider some of these in the next section.

WHAT TO CONSIDER WHEN CHOOSING A DISTRIBUTED CACHING OR DATA GRID PRODUCT ?

The following shopping list should give an indication of the kinds of questions to ask when considering a DataGrid for your applications:

❏ What topologies / patterns does it support ?

❏ How does it High Availability and Resilience ?

❏ What management and monitoring features does it have?

❏ Which languages and interfaces does the API support (.Net, C++, Map (JSR-107), JMS, JDBC)

❏ Does it support versioning of data items?

- ❏ What is the transactional throughput speed and how does it perform on put/get actions?

- ❏ What is the proven and expected Scale at which it function before noticeable or significant degradation?

- ❏ Where is it rolled out in production, at what size and what function is it performing?

- ❏ Does it have a downloadable test framework available?

- ❏ Does it connect with any third party applications (grid solutions for example), out of the box?

- ❏ Which replication strategies does it support?

- ❏ Are there sufficient authentication and security features (does it Integrate with Identity management systems)?

- ❏ Is there support for Multi-tenancy?

- ❏ What are the available data locking strategies

- ❏ What is the maximum number of simultaneous clients that can connect?

- ❏ What are Network requirements (for example does it have Unicast and multicast support)?

- ❏ Are you planning this to be a Read Mostly, Read Write or Write Mostly cache ?

- ❏ Think about the features you need now and the future

- ❏ Does it support Collections, Lease Management, SQL and Continuous queries.

This list is not comprehensive, and certainly not specific to your application, but it does highlight key points to consider.

OPEN SOURCE CHOICES

Apart from the three main DataCache vendors there are a number of open source offerings that could be considered to address your caching needs. It depends very much on the requirements you have, and the degree of support you require. The main ones are listed below with a very brief description.

EHCACHE[47]

This is a pure Java, in-Process Cache that acts as a pluggable cache to Hibernate 2.1. It features include memory and disk stores, replication, cache listeners and cache loaders. It supports both JSR-107 and the JCACHE API, and the largest installations use hundreds of caches which store gigabytes of data. Commercial support is available for various aspects of the product.

BERKLEYDB[48]

This is a lightweight and flexible computer software library that provides a high-performance embedded database, with bindings in C, C++, Java, Perl, Python Ruby, Tcl and many more. It is often used alongside compute grid.

It does not support SQL or any other query language, nor does it support table schema or table columns. A program accessing the database is free to decide how the data is to be stored in a record.

Berkley DB is now supported and owned by Oracle.

CACHE4J[49]

Is a Cache for Java Objects, with a simple API that is designed for multi-threading. It implements synchronized cache reads and

---

[47] http://ehcache.sourceforge.net/

[48] http://www.oracle.com/technology/products/berkeley-db/index.html

[49] http://cache4j.sourceforge.net/

writes and a variety of cache eviction methodologies. Still under development it has no provenance in any large scale environment.

SWARMCACHE[50]

A Simple Distributed Cache which is Optimised for Read Only, designed for clustered web applications. It can only use the multicast protocol, which may be an issue for some environments. It supports Hibernate and JPOX.

JCACHE[51]

This is the Reference implementation of JSR-107, a stable standard distributed Map interface. It uses the Space concept, implemented as a simplified JavaSpaces API sitting on top of a high performance message bus. Performance is improved through an architectural approach that allows efficient parallel, independent, multi-threading to ensure that each object is processed in an optimized way. SEDA[52] (Staged Event Driven Architecture) is the basis of message bus toolkits such as Mule and was designed as a robust high performance platform for internet services.

JCache offers an in-JVM cache, with full transactional support, and a clustered cache which replicates state across clusters of JVM's using the Space abstraction.

MEMCACHED[53]

MemCacheD was originally developed by Danga Interactive for LiveJournal, but is now used by many large sites, such as Facebook, YouTube, Twitter, Dig etc. It is an In Memory Hash table designed for speeding up web applications which

---

[50] http://swarmcache.sourceforge.net/

[51] http://activespace.codehaus.org/JCache

[52] http://www.eecs.harvard.edu/~mdw/proj/seda/

[53] http://www.danga.com/memcached/

implements a simple read-through functionality to take load off of the database. It is simple and straightforward, but lacks any kind of security or authentication.

MemcacheD can be distributed across multiple machines. And it uses a LRU (Least Recently Used) policy for evicting data when the cache gets full.

TERRACOTTA[54]

Terracotta's core product is Terracotta Distributed Shared Objects (DSO). It provides object clustering services to Java applications by enabling objects created locally (running in a JVM) to become available to applications running in other JVM's (in a cluster`).   It is not strictly a data cache although it uses a Network Attached Memory (NAM) technology to manage data. It provides clustering services transparently via a plug-in to the JVM. Basically this enables a Java developer using Terracotta to writes multi-threaded Java applications if they were writing to a single JVM. Once complete they can deploy it on a Terracotta-enabled JVM cluster. This allows, to a certain level, the developer to view the JVM cluster as one single large JVM.

Terracotta can integrate with EHCache as well as other caching technologies and it can be used as a cache in its own right through using a map as the interface although there is a need to implement a queue and separate thread for flushing changes to the map asynchronously to the database

It is possible to make use of the Terracotta WorkManager framework to achieve scaled out IMDG, although there is still a need to flush changes to the DB from the queue.

---

54   http://www.terracotta.org/

BEST PRACTICE

Here we suggest some basic principles and the sorts of things that should be considered when designing an IMDG solution and picking a product. Of course, the final choice very much depends on the specific needs of your application.

Pick the correct topology

Picking the correct caching topology for the Grid can mean the difference between failure and success. Make sure you understand all aspects of the use case and ensure you involve the vendor at this stage.

Design for failure.

What happens if the Compute node fails? What happens if any part of the distributed cache infrastructure fails? What happens if the hardware fails?

Consider these issues around compute and data grid integration

If compute power is the limiting resource then a Compute Grid is needed and the following need to be considered:

❏ **Scalability** – Of course the ultimate scalability is through implementing a peer to peer cache, but this brings with it issues around consistency of data, or worse locking of the entire cache while transactional data is updated. To alleviate this we can consider partitioning of data into cache regions and using a partitioned topology with or without peer-to-peer cache replication.

❏ **Consistency** – There is clearly a tension between consistency and scalability. In order to ensure the data is fully consistent each operation should be transactional and in a large-scale system this can have disastrous effects. It is important to ask up front the following questions:

- Does every compute task have to have the same data available?

- if one task writes data to the store, does every node need that data (transactions)

❏ **Low latency** - for really low latency the data and compute task need to be co-located. This can be achieved through ensuring a good locality of reference and making use of data/ compute affinity available in the compute grid vendor solutions. Ultimately an embedded cache, or near cache makes access faster, but again at the cost of consistency.

Multi-tenancy

This is the notion, which is becoming much more prevalent now, of running a single service on the same hardware for many customers. In an internal data grid each customer would be a business line or data consumer. In some sectors, such as finance, data cannot be shared across Chinese walls in the same company and so it is essential to take steps that ensure isolation and security of data.

SUMMARY

In this chapter we have introduced caching, and IMDG's, reviewed topologies, vendors, open source candidates and suggested what you should look at when selecting and IMDG vendor as well as some suggestion around best practices. This should more than enable you to have a sensible conversation with anyone about distributed data caching and in-memory data grids.

Virtualisation and Orchestration

Virtualisation itself is not a new concept but it was only a few years ago that it really broke into the mainstream, finding initial success in providing development and test environment and associated cost savings. Despite initial resistance, Virtualisation is now being used successfully in production systems and is now not only a viable alternative, but, in some cases, is the only way to create the scale, flexibility and value required of the of physical environment.

One key advantage of virtualisation is that fundamentally it is a software solution, and as such it is easy to copy, modify and distribute virtual instances (VM's) across the environment. Automated approaches to doing this fall into the category of Orchestration, and in fact for the enterprise Orchestration and Virtualisation go hand in hand. This chapter deals with these concepts.

WHAT IS VIRTUALISATION?

Virtualisation and Emulation are often compared, but there are a set of important differences. Emulation provides the functionality of a target processor completely in software. The main advantage being that you can emulate one type of processor on any other type of processor. Unfortunately it tends to be slow. Virtualisation however involves taking a physical processor and partitioning it into multiple contexts. All of which take turns running directly on the processor itself. Because of this, Virtualization in faster than emulation.

Virtualization introduces an abstraction layer on top of resources, so that physical characteristics are hidden from the user. This abstraction layer takes care of resource allocation in order to meet the needs of the applications being run. In essence virtualisation enables you to create one or more virtual machines that can run simultaneously at the same time as the host operating system. In its early days virtualisation was more specialised and was utilised specifically in a vendor-controlled way, such as IBM's LPAR approach for example. Virtualization vendors claim consolidation ratios of 4, with the potential for making available up to 75 percent of new infrastructure available in a data center.

Chipset manufacturers are now optimising the processors to support virtualisation. Both Intel and AMD have extended the instruction sets of their newer processors to give increased support for virtualisation. 'AMD-V' is what AMD have labelled their technology and Intel's technology is called 'VT.' Expect even further advances. For example the Intel Xeon 7400 Dunnington processors that launched in September 2008 include something called FlexMigration. This allows virtual machines to be moved around easily in a server pool. We would advise that you understand in detail the processors that your virtual Grid runs upon as they offer a key mechanism for optimization.

Key to the virtualisation architecture is the hypervisor, the virtual machine manager. A hypervisor is a program that allows multiple operating systems to share a single hardware host. Although each operating system appears to have the host's processor, memory, and other resources all to itself, the hypervisor is actually controlling the host processor and resources. It allocates what is needed to each operating system in turn, and these allocations can be managed and tuned.

There are two types of Hypervisor:

❑ **Type 1:** This is referred to as a bare-metal or native hypervisor. This type of hypervisor is software based and runs directly on a specific hardware and hosts a guest operating system. XEN, VMware ESX, Parallels Server, Hyper-V all have examples of this type of hypervisor.

❑ **Type 2:** This type of hypervisor runs within an actual operating system. VMware Server (GSX), VirtualBox, Parallels Workstation and Desktop are examples of this type of hypervisor. The Type 2 Hypervisor is typically people are referring to when they think of Virtualisation.

There is a third element: *Paravirtualisation.* This is when the Operating System has been modified to be aware of the Hypervisor that is running. This makes the interaction and integration between the two much smoother and in theory less prone to any errors that may be generated. 'Enlightenment" in Windows Server 2008 is an example of this as it enables the OS to interact directly with the Hypervisor.

With computing resources at a premium in terms of space, power, location, and cost, the use of virtualised Grid infrastructures is a very compelling proposition for existing servers and hardware that are under utilised or have spare capacity cycles. Virtualisation can actually be thought of as addressing one of the deficiencies of building a Grid infrastructure, that of resource. It also addresses differences in OS infrastructure, software stacks etc. With virtualisation, on-demand deployment of pre-configured virtual machines containing all the software required by a job is possible. Flexibility is also added to resource management and application execution. For example running virtual machines can be controlled by freezing them (similar to check-pointing) or by migrating them in a real-time scenario while keeping the virtualised Grid running

Indeed this proposition can is beginning to be thought of as a 'private cloud', in which virtualisation is used to deliver Grid enabled services across an organisation and in which best practices utilised in 'public clouds' are used to deliver this. As we shall discuss the virtualisation providers are releasing products and tools to enable the deployment and management of private clouds.

There are also drawbacks to watch out for. When you communicate 'to' and 'from' a virtualized node, the packets needs to pass through the virtualised communications layer. This is an overhead and you should estimate between 10-20% of a performance hit for this. Furthermore the VM is not an indication of the speed or performance of your grid. For example running four virtual machines on a 4 core 4-GHz chip is not the same as having 4 & 1Ghz dedicate chips for each VM. Also when one of your virtual machines is idle, if other VM's are co-hosted they will get the majority of the power.

As the machines are virtual, and using resource cycles that are not in use, you may find that certain nodes are not available when you need or expect them. To this end you should ensure you have the ability to burst when required and have virtualised management infrastructure in place to handle this.

Virtualisation standards

Very few standards have existed in the virtualisation space although efforts have been made fairly recently. Under the banner of the Distributed Management Task Force, new specifications created by Dell, HP, IBM, Microsoft, VMware and XenSource provide hope for comprehensive industry standards.

The vendor drafted Open Virtual Machine Format[55] (OVF) doesn't aim to replace existing formats, but instead ties them together in a standards-based XML package that contains all the necessary installation and configuration parameters. This, in theory, will allow any virtualization platform (that implements the standard) to run the virtual machines. We are already seeing vendors within the virtualisation space adopt this standard. Indeed the VMware vCloud has a concept of vApps which could contain one or more virtual machines. The Open Virtual Machine format specification defines a vApp encapsulation. i.e. at some point one will be able to buy a vApp in OVF form from other vendors.[56]

The features / benefits of OVF are:

❑ Simple user experience – streamlined installation

❑ Optimised Distribution – portability and compression of virtual appliances

❑ Vendor and Platform independence

❑ Extensibility – specification that can be extended

❑ Localisation – independent of the virtual appliance

❑ Supports appliance solution stacks – more than one virtual appliance

From a Grid perspective virtualisation standards can only be a good thing as they protect from vendor lock in and make migration and mixed utilisation easier.

---

[55] Find out more about OVF at http://www.dmtf.org/home
[56] http://virtualization.com/video-audio-vodcast-vlog/2008/09/16/dmtf-releases-ovf-version-1-0/

Using Amazon EC2

Many organisations are used to using virtualisation in-house probably from the use of VMware. Often the organisational need is to move an existing virtualised application hosted on VMware to a cloud provider, such as EC2. If this is your scenario, standards won't help but you can still achieve what you need to do. The basic steps to do this are:

1. Shut down the existing VMware image
2. Grab a copy of QEMU[57], which you can use to convert the image.
3. The VMDK file will then be converted into a RAW file
4. As this is a RAW image it should be bootable by a local Xen, QEMU or KVM installation.
5. Now you need to bundle this into an AMI using 'ec2-bundle-image'
6. Lastly you need to upload the bundled image and register it in EC2.
7. The AMI will appear when you request a list of your images

It is also worth pointing out that vendors already provide a mechanism to move from one hypervisor to another. For example Parallels with their 'transporter' utility and VMware with their 'importer' tool. Other companies also provide management and conversion products such as RPath and Cohesive FT.

The Globus Alliance provides the concept of 'Virtual Workspaces'. These provide services with interfaces to Virtual Machine management functions. These are based on the WSRF[58] protocol. A Workspace is a combination of the meta-data

---

[57] http://bellard.org/qemu/

[58] Web Services Resouce Framework, is an OASIS Web services specification outlining how to model, access and interact with stateful resources via Web services.

and a resource allocation request. Currently XEN is the only virtualisation technology that is supported, and this only works with the Globus Grid initiative.

VIRTUALISATION PROVIDERS

There are many virtualisation providers and we could write a separate book outlining and discussing them all We have therefore restricted ourselves to look at the major ones you may encounter.

XEN

The Xen virtualisation product is now around 5 years old and was originally started by the Systems Research Group at Cambridge in the UK. Originally part of the Xenoserver project, the ethos behind it was to provide a distributed network of operating system environments tailored to the users needs. It's not hard to see the overlap and similarities with Grid

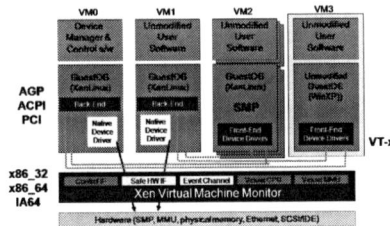

Figure 14 - Xen

XEN is a cross platform, supporting many operating systems, and is probably the closest thing to a standard from a Virtual Machine Hypervisor perspective. Although Citrix purchased it in 2007 for $500 million there is still an Open Source entry version[59], which at the time of writing is at version 3.3. Many vendors base their virtualisation architecture on top of XEN. This includes Citrix, Red Hat, SUSE, Virtual Iron, and many other who OEM it. Perhaps the most important value proposition offered by XEN is its low initial cost i.e. "free" if you use the open source edition.

There is a big cross over between Cloud technologies and virtualisation, with virtualisation infrastructures key to being able to deliver Cloud infrastructures. To that end Citrix have recently announced the 'Citrix Cloud Centre 'also referred to as 'C3'. This provides a portfolio of tools that can automate VM deployment, VM movement, and VM SLA management. It bundles together Citrix XenServer Virtual Infrastructure, Netscaler application switch, WANScaler access gateway and bandwidth optimizer, and the forthcoming Workflow Studio for application self-provisioning and admin orchestration. There is no doubt this will be a major player in providing private cloud infrastructures and management tooling for Grid topologies. This offering competes directly with VMware's VCloud.

SOLARIS ZONES

Solaris Zones are a software partitioning technology used to virtualise operating system services and provide an isolated and secure environment for running". Zones, were developed under the code name "Kevlar," and the design ethos of zones was that rather than load a whole operating system into a physical or logical partition, zones abstract the essential things that make a partition different i.e. resource, fault and security isolation, from the Solaris operating kernel and various system services such as file systems and create a new kind of logical partition.

---

[59]   www.xen.org

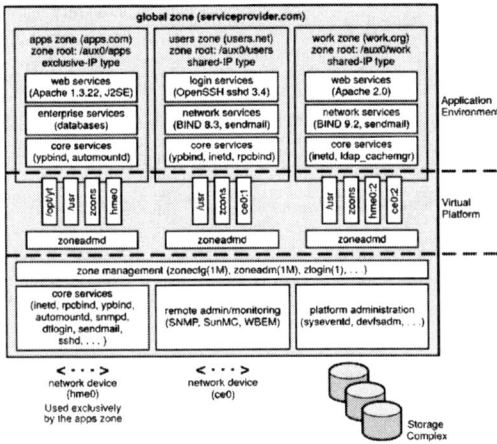

Figure 15 - Solaris Zones

Essentially the important components of the Solaris OS, are shared, read-only, through a loop-back FS to each zone, which means that you only have one OS to maintain despite having multiple virtual OS's available to you. Multiple /etc conf files and applications are local to each zone. This means when you apply a patch you can do it once rather than for each virtualised OS. You can also do things like share a directory to each zone read-only or even a directory that is read-write to zone or to only certain zones.

Each of the zones is completely unaware of the other zones. Each application appears to be on a completely separate machine from the rest. Resource management allows you to control the QoS for each virtual OS. Remember, this is all out of the box, no special add-ons or anything is needed, and it takes a few minutes to setup a zone. Things are divided and jailed at the kernel level, so even if one zone is compromised it does not affect the other zones. If a zone crashes it does not affect the other zones or the global zone. And at the global zone level you can see everything going on in each zone. This is very different to things like LPAR's and nPartitions as they require a local install of the OS in each virtual machine.

Zones however do not automatically manage resources . For that you need resource pools. A resource pool can be created with its own dedicated CPU resources and scheduling class. One or more zones can be bound to the pool to take advantage of those resources. Processor sets (PSets) can be created and associated with each pool where it is important to dedicate CPUs to a pool.

There is also some work on tightly integrating zones with Solaris Grid Engine via Project Berlin. In this scenario an execution daemon running in the global zones would round-robin jobs into the known non-global zones. If you are evaluating or running Sun Grid Engine you should investigate Zones more thoroughly.

IBM LPAR

LPAR is an acronym for *Logical Partitioning.* It enables computers resources, such as CPU. Memory, and storage to be split into smaller units and run with its own instance of an OS and applications. IBM first introduced logical partitions in 1976. Both IBM's S/390 (now z/900 Series) and AS/400 products support logical partitioning. Hitachi and Sun Microsystems also use forms of logical partitioning, as well as Microsoft that supports DLPAR's – dynamic logical partitions.

LPAR enables total partitioning at the hardware level and also offers virtualisation at perhaps even a greater granularity than is available today elsewhere. New domains can be created dynamically, given virtual CPUs (a real CPU or a percentage of one), slots of memory and access to shared disk channels. All the disk storage and storage connections can be shared (a feature called EMIF) between LPARs. Configuration work can be done whilst the LPARs is up and running.

It is possible to construct a mainframe based Grid system using

LPAR's. This is valuable because mainframe systems provide a level of isolation and security that often takes a lot of work to achieve on alternative infrastructures. Logical partitions on zOS means there is no leakage of not only information resource, but also execution resources between the different partitions. On alternative virtual infrastructures grid tasks normally run as separate processes within the operating system, and therefore share resources controlled by the underlying Operating System. Unlike the LPAR approach this could result in corruption of the data of one task by another task.

Figure 16 - IBM Virtualisation Engine

It is likely that such a system would use the Globus toolkit or the IBM Grid Toolbox which is a commercial derivative of the Globus toolkit, that provides support for interoperability between z series and p series processors.

VIRTUAL BOX

Sun acquired Virtual Box when they acquired the German open source vendor Innotek, which had released Virtual Box under the GPL. This makes Virtual Box the only professional solution that is freely available as Open Source Software under the terms of the GNU General Public License (GPL). Just like VMware, Microsoft and Citrix, Sun wanted to offer a broad set of virtualization software. Virtual Box supports Mac, Linux, Windows, Solaris,

Open Solaris and OS/2 as guess operating systems.

Sun is promoting Virtual Box under the xVM brand. And 'Virtual Box' is the entry-level product under this banner. The other three are xVM Server, an enterprise grade bare metal hypervisor; xVM Ops Center, the management framework, and Sun VDI 2.0, which provides remote consolidation of desktop operating systems.

Virtual Box has some nice features which includes virtual Machine Disk Format (VMDK[60]) support which allows VirtualBox to use disk images created in VMware, and Public API which support Java, Python, SOAP and XPCOM. This can be used to control VM configuration and execution.

If you are using Solaris, Globus and the N1 Grid Engine then you should check the latest status of virtual box and its integration with this Grid tooling.

PARALLELS

Parallels is a US based virtualisation company that is better know for its virtualisation products for the Apple Mac Platform. It offers Desktop, Workstation and a Server product and competes directly with VMware. It also offers Parallels Virtuozzo Containers. This is an operating system-level virtualization product that is designed for large-scale server environments and data centers. The likelihood is that if you have used a shared hosting environment then you may have inadvertently used this technology.

Parallels is a private company and to our experience has not made inroads in the enterprise domain with its software, particularly in Grid environments.

---

[60]VMDK is VMware's proprietary VM format

VMWARE

VMware was formed in 1998 in the United States. It's name is an amalgam of "Virtual Machine" and 'software'. EMC bought VMware for $625m in 2004 and three years later floated 10 percent of the virtualization company in a partial IPO, which generated $1 billion. Once could argue that VMware started the current virtualisation movement when it targetted IT directors that wanted to consolidate their servers. VMware's ESX hypervisor proved to be a tool that could do just that.

VMware is available in 3 versions:

❏ **VMWare Workstation** – This is the basic VMware environment. It works with Linux , Windows and more recently Mac environments. This includes desktop and server Products. It is,designed primarily as a desktop solution. It has limited performance and virtual machine management tools and it's not really designed for the long-term execution of a server or other environments.

❏ **VMware GSX Server** – GSX Server is designed to work on as a hosting environment for virtual servers. Unlike the Workstation product GSX Server works only with server operating systems. GSX server includes extensive control and management systems to enable partitioning of the host CPU, RAM, and disk times effectively.

❏ **VMware ESX Server** – ESX is a complete virtual hosting environment. It doesn't use a host operating system as it acts as the operating system itself. This provides better all-around performance, because you get full virtualization without the host Operating System overhead. Be aware that it requires very high-specification of hardware which includes a minimum of 2 CPUs, 2 network interfaces, and a storage device that implements RAID. It has a 17MB footprint.

Recently VMware announced the availability of ESXi, which is a free version of their virtual hosting environment. This is attractive but you should understand the trade offs of using this for your Grid environment. The main differences seem to be:

❑ Smaller set of certified hardware

❑ Cannot mange ESXi via serial cable

❑ No support for Netqueue (boosts Ethernet 10G performance)

❑ VMware and Mellanox Technologies supports Infiniband host channel adapters on ESX., but ESXi does not support this.

❑ The ESXi kernel is missing jumbo frames support in TCP/IP stack (allows to send larger frames out onto physical network)

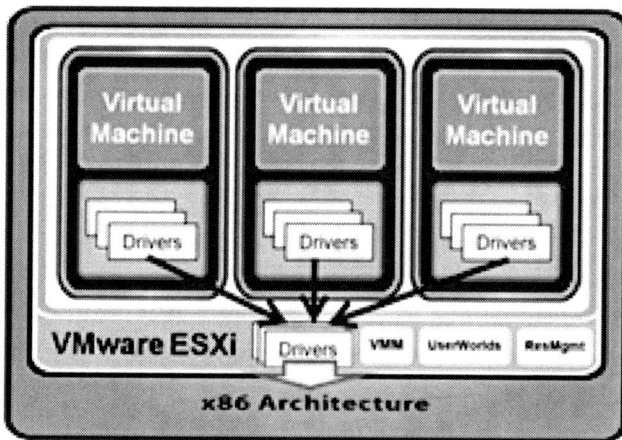

Figure 17 - VMware

VMware dispute that applications run slower in a virtual environment and they offer a number of interesting studies on performance on their website and blogs. There are some interesting tuning tips that you should investigate and take advantage of if you are interested in using VMware with your Grid.

VMware announced their vCloud offering in 2008. The idea behind vCloud is similar to that of the Citrix cloud offering that it is to deliver the security, availability and compatibility with incumbent VMware hypervisor technology. VMware is promoting this as VDC-OS or 'Virtual Data center OS'. This will be made up of vServices for availability, security, scalability and infrastructure vServices which will be formed of vComputer, vStorage, and vNetwork. VMware's management tools will evolve into VMware vCenter that will provide management services for application management as well as infrastructure management.

Why could VCloud and the Citrix Cloud offering be important to Grid Computing? We started off this chapter by suggesting that one of the deficiencies of Grid Computing was that of resource. For grid computing to take hold on a broader scale there is a need for a new layer of federated abstraction for coordinating all the connected pieces of hardware and a simple interface that hides the network's complexities from users. These are the ambitious standards that Citrix, VMware and a host of other vendors have set themselves to achieve.

MICROSOFT HYPER V

Microsoft had long been involved in the virtualisation world with Virtual PC and so it has some sort of pedigree as a virtualisation vendor, although virtualisation perhaps goes against its ethos of selling more software OS licenses.

It released Hyper-V in early 2008 and this provides support for:

- x86 and x64 editions of Windows Server 2008

- Windows Server 2003

- Windows 2000 Server SP4

- Windows HPC Server 2008

- SUSE Linux Enterprise Server 10 SP1/SP2

❑ Windows Vista SP1 (except Home editions)

❑ Windows XP Professional SP2/SP3/x64

❑ Windows Server 2008 guests

❑ Windows HPC Server 2008

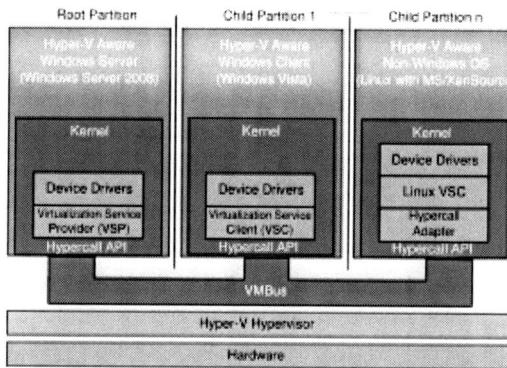

Figure 18 - Microsoft HyperV

Hyper-V is installed directly onto server hardware, enabling it to host multiple virtual machines in logically separate partitions. The primary has to run Windows Server 2008. This is referred to as the *paravirtualization* method, which requires the operating system be modified to run as a virtual machine. This makes the footprint around 2.6 GB.

Many OS platforms are not supported such as Redhat Linux, Mac OSX / Leopard, Ubuntu etc. This makes Hyper V more attractive to those who have an investment in Windows in their data center or architecture, as Hyper-V is fully dependent on Windows 2008.

DATASYNAPSE FABRIC SERVER

FabricServer is DataSynapse's platform that is aimed at spreading applications across clusters of servers. This is described by DataSynapse as 'application virtualisation' and it is aimed at achieving much the same as standard server virtualization but doesn't have to involve multiple Operating Systems. Its aim is to combine multiple servers into one large computing resource, whereas traditional virtualization is mostly concerned with dividing up a single server.

Fabric Server requires all servers to be identically configured and to have every required application installed on each, together with the Fabric Server software. This then provides load balancing with combined management utilities. Load balancing distributes requests to the appropriate server while the management utility allows administrators to divide the total compute capacity between the installed applications.

This approach makes an IT infrastructure more flexible though it doesn't help much with consolidation. A disadvantage is that the DataSynapse software needs to be able to support every application it manages which means that it may not work with everything. Possibly the greatest benefits can be achieved when using it with virtual machines, as FabricServer allows multiple OS images to be installed and managed.

DataSynapse recently announced (August 2008) that it is integrating its FabricServer management tool with VMware VirtualCenter. The integration will enable IT managers to provision, monitor and manage their virtual data centers through a single console.

PLATFORM EGO[61]

Platform were using the term Orchestration for a number of years before it became fashionable. Their EGO product is central to their re-engineering of Symphony but is a stand alone Orchestration product. It sits as a virtual operating system on top

---

[61] http://www.platform.com/Products/platform-enterprise-grid-orchestrator

of a cluster and is able to allocate resources Dynamically across the cluster, based upon demand. This provides an alternative to grid for resource sharing that is non intrusive with a set of policy based allocation tools to ensure the management of SLA's. Because of the open architecture, through plug-ins both Platform tools (LSF, Symphony) and bespoke tools can be orchestrated through EGO. This product is certainly capable of providing the infrastructure for an internal cloud.

LIQUID LABS VSCAPE[62]

VScape, the orchestration product from LiquidLabs provides demand and time based dynamic allocation of resources. Originally built with adapters for the main grid and Data Grid vendors it now provides adapters for orchestrating Virtual Machines. Liquid Labs concept of Liquid Compute is that applications dynamically tune themselves in line with the SLA's assigned to them. Their route-map includes a full internal and external cloud solution.

SUMMARY

It is clear that virtualised computing infrastructure is an important part of Grid computing and whether architected in a local data center or outsourced, virtualisation can provide a fundamental capability for the development of a flexible and scalable foundation for modern Grid infrastructures. For making processors, storage and networking assets more widely available and usable by Grid software applications, virtualisation is a key technology. Benefits include increased utilisation, greater flexibility, better use and scale of existing capacity whilst reducing costs and getting a better ROA[63] for the business.

---

[62] http://www.liquidlabs.co.uk/
[63] Return on Asset

There are still many challenges that have to be addressed when using virtualisation and Grid environments such as security. For example, if the virtual images are used from a pre-existing repository, malicious software or code could potentially be installed on the image. Also Grid schedulers/ brokers are not, 'out of the box', able to perform management operations on the virtual machines, such as suspending, resuming, checkpointing and migrating them for example. There are many other things to consider, but what we are starting to see is that the Cloud Computing Domain, Virtualisation Domain, and the Grid Domain are converging on solutions to these problems. We can see this in the recent initiatives from Citrix and VMware with their Cloud Centre and vCloud offerings, and we will discuss this further in the chapter dedicated to Cloud Computing.

Clouds on the Horizon

Cloud Computing's stock has risen rapidly in the last 12 months and is set to rise even further as a result of the on-demand pay-for-what-you-use economic model of cloud computing. Especially given the current state of the global economy.

Gartner predicted that despite the current economy woes, online software revenue will have surpassed $6.4-billion US in 2008 and is expecting the market to more than double by 2012, with annual revenue predictions of $14.8-billion.

We can trace the rise of the Cloud Computing model from the early ASP or Application Service Provider Model that surfaced at the end of the 1990's. This transitioned into the SaaS or Software-as-a-Service Model, which itself has lent itself as a model to Cloud Computing. There are many definitions of Cloud computing, but we particularly like the one sentence definition by RightScale CEO Michael Crandall who defines Cloud Computing as:

> *"... providing easily accessible compute and storage resources on a pay-as-you-go, on-demand basis, from a virtually infinite infrastructure managed by someone else."*[64]

We would like to draw attention to the 'infinite infrastructure' that

---

64

http://www.informationweek.com/news/services/hosted_apps/showArt icle.jhtml?articleID=210602225

Michael talks about. It is this scalable or elastic nature of the clouds and the ability to be able to do this on demand that has attracted the attention of everyone from startup's to blue chip enterprises.

A CLOUD OF ACRONYMS

When discussing Cloud Computing one can easily get lost in a soup of acronyms. We define the key terms below.

SaaS (Sofware-as-a-Service) The core proposition of SaaS is the delivery of multi-tenant services from a remote location over an Internet Protocol network via a subscription or outsourcing based contract. The consumer of the service could be another service. The service could be hosted in a cloud or in a more traditional network data centre with pre-provisioned capacity. Examples include Salesforce.com, WebEx, Zoho and Go to Meeting. End of year predictions for SaaS in the enterprise in 200s are for a 27% growth.[65]

IaaS (Infrastructure-as-a-Service): This is also often referred to as HaaS (hardware-as-a-service). IaaS provides IT resources (processing power, storage, data center space, services, compliance) on-demand, enabling the IT organisation to bill on a utility computing basis for the amount of resources consumed

PaaS (Platform-as-a-Service): PaaS is a programming or programmable platform often presented as a RIA (Rich Internet Application). PaaS offers a faster, more cost-effective model for application development and delivery. PaaS provides all the infrastructure needed to run applications over the Internet. Examples are Google AppEngine, and Force.com.

DaaS (Data-as-a-Service): DaaS is a type of SaaS that provides access to a set of set of aggregated data stored external to an

---

[65] http://www.gartner.com/it/page.jsp?id=783212

organisation. It is also starting to become known as Database-as-a-Service in which the DataBase lives in, and can be accessed from, the Cloud. Oracle's recent announcement about putting Oracle 11g in the cloud is an example of this.

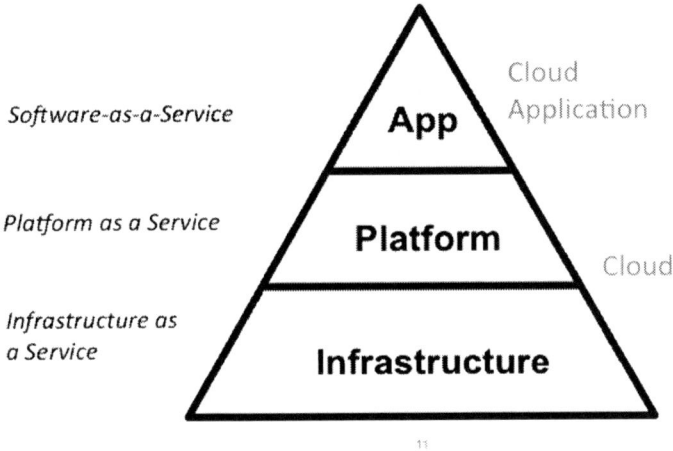

Figure 19 - Acronym soup

ARE CLOUD AND GRID THE SAME ?

One of the things we should address is the question of whether cloud computing is just Grid computing in another guise. As usual the answer is not a straightforward one, as it really depends on the context.

As we outlined above Cloud Computing is an umbrella term for a whole heap of technologies of which Grid Computing is only one. However the vision of being able to process large amounts of information, scale predictably, have greater compute power available, shorten compute cycles, gaining greater flexibility is definitely similar.

More importantly the world of Grid and Cloud are intermeshed in the similar challenges that they face, he need of management for large compute clusters, the ability to interoperate with virtualisation, have standardised discovery mechanisms, API's and scheduler.

In our opinion there is one key difference between Grid Computing and Cloud computing - Virtualisation. Every Cloud solution today is pinned together by some form of virtualisation technology. As we discuss in the virtualisation chapter, virtualisation is making huge inroads into Grid Computing but it is not yet a pre-requisite.

Forester defines two types of *Clouds* that exists within Cloud Computing:[66]

❑ *Server Clouds:* Which deal with the needs of traditional business applications

❑ *Scale Out Clouds:* Which differ from Server clouds in that one of the tenets is that they need to support larger workloads such as those required for Grid Computing.

For the purposes of this chapter on we are interested in the latter which have an impact on HPC and Grid Computing

Rich Wolski from the Euclayptus project made an interesting observation[67] on the differences between Grid computing and Cloud Computing. He stated that Grid Computing was mostly used 'in environments where users make few but large allocation requests.' He gave an example of a 'lab that may have a 1000 node cluster and where users make allocations for all 1000, or 500, or 200, etc. As only a few of these allocations can be serviced at a time and others need to be scheduled for when resources are released. This results in sophisticated batch job scheduling algorithms of parallel computations.'

66

http://www.forrester.com/Research/Document/Excerpt/0,7211,47100,00.html

[67] http://blog.rightscale.com/2008/07/

He contrasts this with cloud computing which is more used for lots of small allocation requests. 'For example The Amazon EC2 accounts are limited to 20 servers each by default[68] and lots and lots of users allocate up to 20 servers out of the pool of many thousands of servers at Amazon. The allocations are real-time and in fact there is no provision for queuing allocations until someone else releases resources. This is a completely different resource allocation paradigm, a completely different usage pattern, and all this results in completely different method of using compute resources.'

This is an interesting view and it is true that the Grid world is primarily (although not wholly) focussed around batch job scheduling, whereas Clouds are much more oriented towards dynamic, real-time allocation. However we are convinced that the world is moving towards interoperability between the two and the gap between the two is shrinking every day. For example we can expect to see lease-based resource provisioning start to become integral to the Grid Scheduler instead of a side effect as Grid Vendors move their product to the Cloud. This paradigm has been central to the Platform EGO layer since 2004, it is a clear direction for DataSynapse and has resulted in the Fabric Server product.

CLOUD INFRASTRUCTURE AND TOOL PROVIDERS

There are many companies delivering cloud platforms and tooling. We will consider some of the main companies that you should evaluate if you are interested in investigating Cloud Computing for your organisation.

---

[68] You can ask Amazon for a larger allocation of servers if you need more than 20

Cloud Platform Providers

IBM

IBM supports Cloud Computing through its Blue Cloud initiative[69]. They have thirteen cloud computing centres and 40 innovation centres globally. In this centres IBM clients can make use of IBM hardware, software and services, but can also leverage the knowledge of 200 dedicated personnel who will help them build and test cloud computing applications and services.

Blue Cloud brings together a gamut of IBM products that are pre-requisites of building a cloud, such as servers, storage, virtualization, service management / provisioning tools and security.

If your company is already significantly invested in IBM as a provider then Blue Cloud may well be worth investigating. System p, x and z servers can be used on Demand to augment compute/ memory resources as needed, along with grid (and many other types) software such as ObjectGrid

AMAZON

Amazon, of all companies, are probably recognised as being at the forefront of SaaS and Cloud computing, being one the first to mass market its platform and storage services wrapped up in a simple, cheap economic model.

The most interesting platform for those interesting in Grid Computing and HPC is EC2, Amazon's Elastic Cloud Platform. Amazon EC2 provides customer-specific Linux instances running in virtual machines. You can decide exactly how powerful you want your virtual hardware. The Virtual machines that you instantiate are rated in EC2 Computer Units (ECUs). Amazon define these as being equivalent to a 1.0GHz to 1.2GHz 2007 Opteron processor.

---

[69] http://www-03.ibm.com/press/us/en/pressrelease/22613.wss

An Amazon Machine Image (AMI) is made up of an operating system and applications you want pre-loaded when the virtual machine is started. You can build the AMI image yourself or Amazon provide a number of pre-built AMI's that you can choose from it's machine image marketplace. [70] These images are either free or charged on pay on demand basis from the provider

Amazon also provides unstructured storage in the form of the Simple Storage Service (S3). This provides basic unstructured remote storage. It is aimed at developers rather than consumers. To developers it exposes objects that can stored in buckets. Services or Applications can do CRUD[71] operations on these objects. This model of use if much more scalable than traditional storage services and can be considered cloud optimised.

Amazon also provides another storage service that it calls SimpleDB. SimpleDB can be considered a slightly different proposition to Amazon S3 as it attempts to bring structured storage in the cloud. SimpleDB organizes not by objects and buckets but in a hierarchy of domains, items, and values. It also provides a query language, although it is not compatible with the most used data query language, SQL.

Amazon has other services such as Simple Queue Service (SQS), which is a way for applications to exchange messages via queues in the cloud. CloudFront is Amazon's Content Delivery Network. It uses Amazon S3 but distributes data out to multiple datacenter locations, ensuring faster access times through low latency file hosting for website users. It is the first consumer-friendly CDN service and holds its own against professional CDN

70

http://developer.amazonwebservices.com/connect/kbcategory.jspa?category ID=101&resultOffset=0&sortField=9&sortOrder=0&filterEntryType ID=-1

[71] CRUD – Create, Read, Update, Delete

services such as CacheFly. You can find more about the other Amazon Cloud Services at http://aws.amazon.com/.

Increasingly Amazon Cloud infrastructure is being viewed as 'Enterprise ready'. This is borne out by the recent announcement of a partnership between the enterprise systems integrator, Cap Gemini, and Amazon for their client base.[72]

A well known case study is the way in which the New York Times used EC2 and Hadoop to generate 11 million article PDF's in 24 hours, using 100 EC2 instances, and generating 1.5 Terrabytes of data in S3. The cost savings were amazing and it is an impressive use of Cloud technology.[73]

From a Grid and HPC perspective there are a number of vendors offerings that can either be found on the EC2 platform, such as GigaSpaces[74] for example. There are also open source offerings available, such as Condor[75], that have been implemented on EC2 but which are not free, although it is possible to build your own Condor AMI image.

The ability to offload Grid compute resource or to be able to handle spikes can be attractive to many organisations, particularly as the alternative can be over provisioning which is expensive. Often the reason quoted for not doing this is security of data. We consider security issues later on in this chapter.

Amazon have recently confirmed that they have extended EC2 to multiple Availability Zones in the Europe to help achieve lower

---

72

http://www.computerweekly.com/Articles/2008/11/21/233513/capgemini-simplifies-the-amazon-cloud.htm

[73] http://www.johnmwillis.com/amazon/the-night-the-nyt-used-hadoop-and-ec2-to-convert-4tbs/

[74] http://www.gigaspaces.com/ec2

[75] http://www.cyclecomputing.com/

latency[76]

Also, C2 is now out of Beta after 2 years and has SLA's equivalents to 99.95% are now in place [77] and this is starting to tempt even larger organisations to look at EC2.

SUN MICROSYSTEMS

Sun has so many technologies offerings for the cloud that at a glance they appear un-coordinated. These offerings include Sun Grid, an on-demand grid computing service that provides access to compute resources from $1 per CPU-hour. It is based on Sun Technologies which include the Sun Grid Engine, and Java. Jobs can be submitted via a scheduler and ran on the grid, the Sun Grid. It is available from network.com. At the time of writing it appears that Sun are taking no new customers although they are continuing to provide a service for existing customers[78]

Sun are directly in the Cloud space offering OpenSolaris on EC2, which includes the ZFS and D-Trace technologies and which can be used with CoolStack[79], a collection of pre-configured optimised applications.

Sun forecasts three type's of cloud

❑ Public Clouds

❑ Private Clouds

❑ Hybrid Clouds

Their aim is to power these clouds and also promote openness and ensure they can promote an alternative to cloud vendor lock-

---

76

http://www.businesswire.com/portal/site/home/permalink/?ndmViewId=news_view&newsId=20081209006582&newsLang=en

77 http://aws.amazon.com/ec2-sla/

78 http://www.theregister.co.uk/2008/12/10/sun_closes_cloud/.

79 http://cooltools.sunsource.net/coolstack/

in

At the beginning of 2009 Sun purchased Q-Layer, a Belgium company, for their Cloud Computing portfolio. The Q-Layer product helps automate the deployment and management of public and private clouds. Q-Layer's technology simplifies cloud management by enabling users to quickly provision and deploy applications.

Sun is promoting itself to be strongly equipped to help the telecommunications vertical and the ISP market to be able to get into the cloud business. It is also focused on helping Small to Medium businesses enter the cloud.

Enterprise enablers for a private cloud are offered through xVM Portfolio[80] which includes Virtual Box (Hypervisor), Ops Centre (discover, provision, update), xVM Server (virtualise servers) and Sun VDI Software (secure virtual desktop access.

HEWLETT PACKARD (HP)

HP's *Flexible Computing Services* provides access to HP owned (or managed) datacenters to run applications and services. Flexible Computing Services is HP's utility computing division. There are a number of services that HP offer though this division:

❑ **Datacenter Transformations**: HP's convert existing none cloud infrastructure into a cloud-based system using a set of their various technologies.

❑ **Performance Optimized Data Center**: This is also know as affectionately as the HP POD. It is a shipping container that can hold 22*19 inch 50u racks. This totals an estimated 3,500 compute nodes (including plus power modules and other backup hardware).

---

[80] http://www.sun.com/software/products/xvm/index.jsp

❑ **Cloud Computing Test Bed**: This is a joint initiative between Yahoo, Intel and HP. The test bed simulates a real-life, global, Internet-scale environment, which gives researchers the ability to test applications and measure the performance of infrastructures and services built to run on large-scale cloud systems.

Many software vendors also take advantage of HP's Flexible Services to be able to offer either test bed's or production environments of applications and services. If your software vendor partners with HP you may be able to take advantage of this.

GOGRID

GoGrid is a Cloud platform provider that offers scalable cloud hosting with an easy to use management interface for rapidly deploying and provisioning servers. It enables the provisioning of Load Balancers along with pre-configured images of applications with multiple Operating System support, including Windows Server. Servers are provisioned using the management console or the REST API. GoGrid has some good features, which include fast deployment of servers, load balancer provisioning, and it is easy to use when scaling applications. It has also announced partnerships with GigaSpaces[81] amongst the grid vendors.

MOSSO

Unlike the other Cloud Computing Platform vendors, Mosso takes a slightly different approach in combining cloud computing with the normal shared-server hosting model. Unique amongst all the vendors is that Mosso does not provide any root access to their severs. Instead It provide servers with operating systems and software pre-installed which is what you would expect to get

---

[81] http://blog.gogrid.com/2008/10/07/gigaspaces-and-gogrid-launch-enterprise-grade-cloud-computing-solution/

from a normal share hosting provider. Mosso believe that this makes it easier to monitor and scale the service on demand and so the client does not need to get involved in installing operating systems. Setting up load balancing, etc. Economically this model appears to be cheaper for the end user with Mosso charging $100 for this HA on demand service.

At the time of writing Mosso have not launched any partnerships with any of the major Grid / DataGrid / HPC Application platform vendors.

FLEXISCALE

FlexiScale is s UK based Cloud Computing Platform vendor, which prices in an on-demand basis for Virtual Private Servers. It is the brainchild of CEO Tony Lucas who also formed XCalibre hosting. It uses XEN for virtualisation and provides support for multiple Operating Systems. It is aimed more at enterprises organisations and it's features support this, and include static IP addressing, an API (and control panel) for the vitualised instances that can clone, copy instances etc. As with all the cloud computing platform vendors it scales on demand (elastic) and it also supports a 99.99% SLA and has persistent storage based on a fully virtualised high-end SAN/NAS back-end.

FlexiScale have formed some impressive partnerships with CohesiveFT, and RightScale amongst the Cloud Computing vendors, and also GigaSpaces amongst the Grid, DataGrid, Application Platform vendors.

Their data-centre is located in the UK so it is likely that it will be more appealing to UK and European customers.

CLOUD TOOL PROVIDERS

RIGHTSCALE

The RightScale Platform is a configuration and management tool, which makes it easier for developers to deploy and control servers and images on different Clouds. Initially, RightScale was only focused in managing applications provided with its own servers that ran on EC2. Since Amazon announced it's own monitoring tools this looked to be a flawed proposition, but RightScale extended their support for managing applications using GoGrid, FlexiScale and RackSpace also. RightScale provides a Dashboard to help manage the infrastructure. The product comes with several price plans, including at the time of writing a free developer account. RightScale use CollectD[82] to provide monitoring and performance measurement facilities.

Alternative Cloud application management companies are WeoCeo and Intridea.

3TERA

3Tera provides software called 'Applogic', a Grid Operating System, which enables an organisation to run its own Private Cloud or Virtual Private Data Center. Essentially an organisation installs the software on commodity-based hardware enabling a self-contained private cloud.

Using AppLogic, applications can be put together using software components called virtual appliances. The virtual appliances form a disposable infrastructure that the application uses when it is enabled. The virtual infrastructure is created dynamically on the grid when the application is run and is then shut down when no longer needed.

3Tera is running in datacenters in seven countries on four continents with additional resources in South America and Australia also coming online.

Many organisations are looking for solutions that they can manage in-house but which also gives them the same flexibility

---

[82] http://www.collectd.org/

and management that public clouds provide. 3Tera is a good option for this.

VMWARE VCLOUD

vCloud aims to help organizations build internal clouds which can also be connected to external clouds. The core of the vCloud offering is a combination of existing, and new, technologies and products from VMware.

Key to the vCloud initiative is the Virtual Datacenter Operating System (VDC-OS). This encompasses:

❑ The pooling of servers, storage and networking resources as a private, "in your own data-center" cloud. This is known as 'infrastructure vServices'

❑ The managing of applications to ensure they get the availability, scalability and security they need. These are known to 'Application vServices'.

❑ The ability to handle interoperability and capacity between private and public (off-premise) clouds. This is known as 'Cloud vServices'. This includes APIs that allow interoperability with another service.

❑ The ability to operate on a utility basis. This is known as 'Vcenter Chargeback"

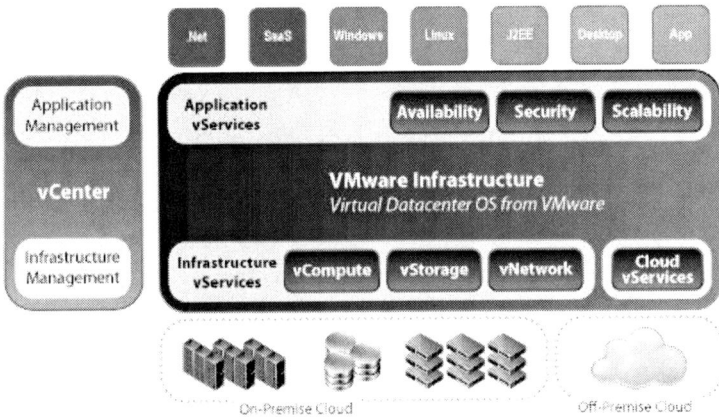

Figure 20 – VMware infrastructure

VMware has a notion to form a "vCloud ecosystem." They already have partners that include Rackspace, Verizon and British Telecom. BT already uses VMware's ESX as part of its virtual datacenter offering.

With most Grid and HPC applications being run inside of private data centers, and many already using virtualisation, the vCloud offering looks set to have a major impact on these environments, from consolidation and resource aggregation to utilising the management and automation features to manage a whole infrastructure.

According to Gartner, private cloud Infrastructures are the future of IT. These private clouds will be based on the flexibility and tooling that are starting to be seen in from the public cloud platform vendors, and a "meta operating system" is needed to manage this which is what VMware are aiming to provide.[83]

COHESIVEFT VPN CUBED

VPN-Cubed by CohesiveFT enables customer-controlled security

---

[83] http://www.networkworld.com/news/2008/111208-private-cloud-networks.html

in a cloud, across multiple clouds, and between the physical data-centre and cloud(s). Using an encrypted cloud VPN[84], the product helps establish a secure bridge between any private infrastructure and the cloud.

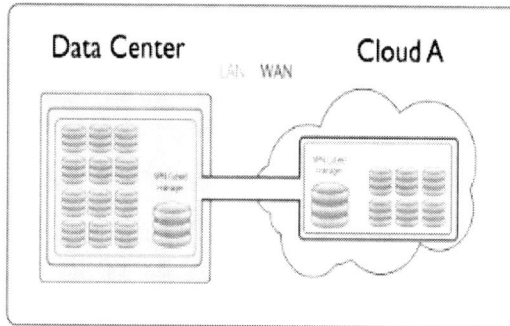

Figure 21- VPNCubed

The differences between a normal VPN and VPN-Cubed is that with VPN-Cubed you are able to securely extend your "internal clouds" in Data-centres to include externally hosted applications / services which in turn run on a Cloud infrastructure that you rent in an on-demand basis. These are highly-available over standard IPSec protocols and are able to accommodate the special dynamic nuances of Clouds such as scaling on demand, and failover between clouds.

At the time of writing VPN-Cubed is the only vendor who provides this type of security for cloud platforms. It currently supports Amazon EC2, Mosso. FlexiScale, and GoGrid.

CohesiveFT also offer an Elastic Server factory where custom server images can be created on demand for a variety of cloud platforms.

---

[84]   Virtual Private Network

GIGASPACES

GigaSpaces provide a unique application platform that provides a combination of Grid / Data Grid and Application Server capabilities. Their in-memory scaling model provides support a variety of API's and languages as we discuss in the DataGrid section, and the core benefits they provide are linear scaling and low latency with a focus on data oriented high throughput applications or services. As all the GigaSpaces data resides in memory and is executed against logic in process, it attacks one of the primary drawbacks of the Cloud, namely that of latency and puts some guarantees and predictability around scaling. It comes with it's own provisioning platform which allow SLA's to be set and acted upon in real-time.

GigaSpaces is available for use on EC2, GoGrid, Joyent, as well as being able to be implemented on private clouds, and also partners with CohesiveFT and RightScale.

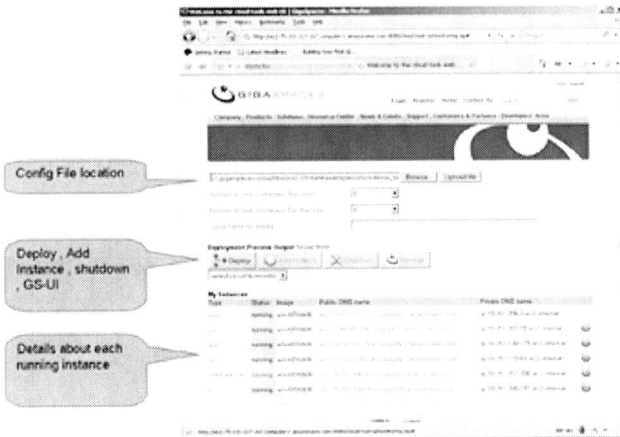

Figure 22 – GigaSpaces Cloud Configuration

EMERGING CLOUD COMPANIES

ZIMORY

Zimory is a below-the-radar start up based in Berlin Germany – spun-off and partially funded by Deutsche Telekom/T-Venture and High-Tech Gruenderfonds.

There are 3 key components to Zimory offerings. Currently, Zimory technology can be used to enable enterprises with large datacenters to manage and more fully utilize servers – in single or multiple locations (Enterprise Cloud). In this capacity, Zimory is one of several options that can accomplish this same task – albeit in different ways. Zimory uses dedicated and not utilized resources from an existing virtualized platform. The internal cloud can thus breath beyond its dedicated resources.

Zimory Marketplace (Public Cloud) combines the benefits of the internal offering with the opportunity for the datacenter (sell-side) to offer excess server capacity in an E-Bay style marketplace to businesses (buy-side) wanting flexibility and cost efficiencies to outsource applications. Currently, some clouds offer this solution on the buy-side with two key differentiators: They offer only their own servers and there is an inherent complexity to both setting up this outsourcing and breaking it down in different clouds.

Zimory provides an interface to connect to a set of divers clouds, which makes the Zimory Marketplace a faster, easier and more cost-effective platform to get access to the best fitting specific cloud for specific enterprise demands.

Lastly, Zimory's *Adaptive Cloud* is the combination of Enterprise and Public Clouds. Adaptive Cloud makes the best use of a company's own server hardware and employ Zimory's Marketplace to access additional resources when needed

Zimory tools combine various types of virtual servers into a single homogeneous computing cloud – enabling dynamic, on-demand movement of applications automatically between servers in one or many locations.

THEFILECLOUD

TheFileCloud is a new service due for imminent release early in 2009. It concentrates on data clouds and offers a single view of aggregated data clouds as well as Cloud Backup, and Public and Private Cloud creation based on their Email-to-Cloud technology.

As storing data in clouds becomes more normal then availability becomes a key issue and the FileCloud offers the ability to have backup data clouds using the same provider or mix and matching providers so that data is always available.

KAAVO

Kaavo provide a J2EE-based cloud management tool for EC2. Kaavo can be used by to launch EC2 server instances, administer permissions to users, transfer files, and perform other administrative tasks. Kaavo is aiming to be cloud platform vendor neutral and is currently working on implementations for FlexiScale and GoGrid. The aim is to enable IT to manage resources across cloud providers form a single Kaavo dashboard. Kaavo is due to be release in early 2009

SCALR

Scalr framework for managing Amazon's EC2 service. Scalr helps enable the "elastic" part of Amazon EC2.

Essentially the Scalr framework is a series of Amazon Machine Images (AMI's) for each of the basic application needs (they comprise an application server, a load balancer, and a database server). A pre-built management suite monitors the load and operating status of the various servers on the cloud. Scalr can then increase / decrease capacity as demand changes. It can also detect and rebuilding images that are not functioning properly.

Scalr is an interesting framework and is an interesting open source alternative to RightScale, WeoCe and Intridea management and monitoring tools.

SOASTA[85]

SOASTA's promotes large scale testing for the Cloud using it's Ajax user interface and promotes the ability to match development speed with test speed. The product is called CloudTest and it is a solution that features both an appliance-based and a cloud-based approach. According to Gartner this is much more suited to organisations real need for cloud right now because not everybody is ready to move wholesale to the cloud and many companies, whatever the size, will prefer a hybrid approach.

SOASTA offer virtual and physical appliances that can be used for everyday functional testing as well as light load testing. Soasta is able to utilise VM's from different platform providers, such as EC2, and also uses these platform providers to simulate load from different geographic locations. Unlike other testing tools the end user application does not move to the cloud. They stay located in their current environment. SOASTA uses the cloud to generate users and then sends them to the application. Load testing peak numbers of users can cast millions of dollars. Using the Soasta cloud it is possible to achieve this as at a fraction of the cost.

Competitors to Soasta include Gomez, which also offers an SaaS testing suite. As the cloud becomes more mature we an expect more testing vendors to adapt their products to work on the cloud.

85

http://www.gartner.com/resources/159300/159303/soasta_is_first_to_bri ng_tes_159303.pdf

VELOCIMETRICS

Velocimetrics are London startup that were spawned from a consultancy company. Although product launch is imminent they were willing to outline what their proposition was for us. Currently the product enables Prime and Secondary Brokers to track the latency in global orders for end to end across the world for each transaction. The product works at a software and a network level.

The company is currently evaluating bringing the product to the cloud environment. Velocimetrics has a visual dashboard which visualises the end to end transaction and the latency that occurs between networks and applications. This product would seem a good fit for companies who are considering bringing latency sensitive applications to the cloud who want to be able to measure / control / understand latency between cloud instances, private and public clouds or public clouds and internal applications etc.

Open source cloud and some options

The open source options around cloud are growing. In this section we touch on a few that we feel are significant for now or the future.

Eucalyptus is an open-source software infrastructure for implementing cloud computing on clusters. The current interface to EUCALYPTUS is compatible with Amazon's EC2 interface, but the infrastructure is designed to support multiple client-side interfaces. It is implemented using commonly available Linux tools and basic Web-service technologies making it easy to install and maintain.

Eucalyptus Architecture: WS-Cloud

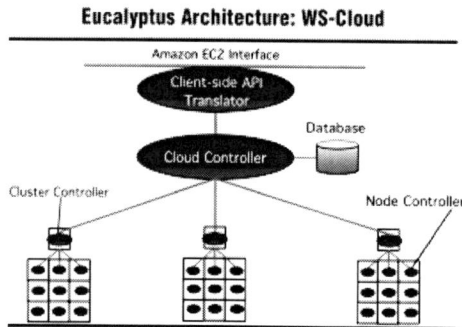

Figure 24 - Project Eucalyptus

Project Caroline is Sun's Open Source Cloud platform. At the moment it is a research project rather than a full product offering. The source code is fully available. Caroline works with Perl, Python, Ruby, PHP, and of course Java. It does not seem to have progressed as much as it should of since it was announced, but provides a full Cloud Computing stack.

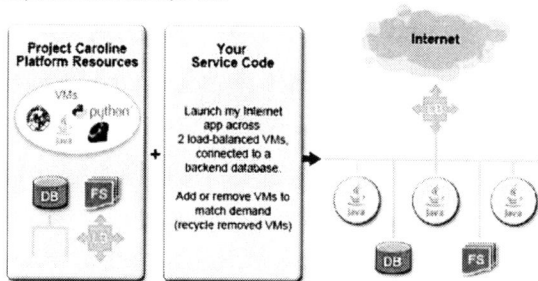

Figure 25 - Project Caroline

Nimbus is an open source toolkit that allows you to turn your cluster into an Infrastructure-as-a-Service (IaaS) cloud. Nimbus also provides an EC2 front-end. This is an implementation of EC2 WSDL that allows you to use clients developed for the real EC2 system against Nimbus based clouds.

Ganglia is not a cloud solution but is exceedingly valuable in monitoring cloud activity. Originally designed for large scale cluster monitoring and deployed on grids and clusters in the tens of thousands of nodes is an exceedingly scalable distributed monitoring system. Ganglia is an open-source project that grew out of the University of California, Berkeley. Ganglia seems tailor

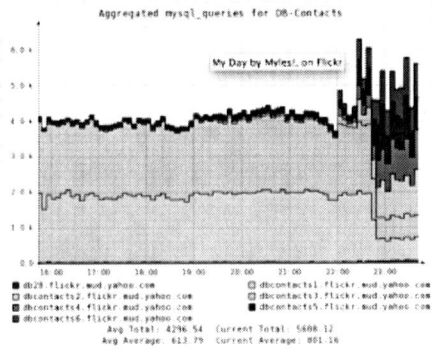

Figure 26 - Ganglia

made for EC2 but can be difficult to setup. Amazon doesn't support multicast on their network, so the default configurations for Ganglia don't work. You can make it work in the cloud using unicast.

ParkPlace is an S3 clone which purports to be a complete implementation of the S3 REST API. it can enable you to have your own private cloud data implementation, but without the ability to scale. Still, useful for testing.

Project Zeppelin has the goal is to provide a consistent, industry standard way to discover, monitor, evaluate and audit the performance of cloud infrastructure / applications across disparate cloud operators. Zeppelin includes a set of agents that provides detailed asset, performance, auditing, benchmarking and usage metering information for cloud infrastructures. It can be deployed remotely, and its data can be securely accessed across the public Internet.

WHY USE THE CLOUD?

There are a number of good reasons for considering cloud computing technology whatever the size and maturity of your organisation. We have listed a number of them here.

Pay-On-Demand - The ability to bring a business model to life using an Enterprise scale solution by being able to pay only for what you use. In many cases Enterprise Software has enterprise price tags so that smaller businesses and individuals have to look at potential OpenSource alternatives. Using Grid and HPC tools on the clouds bridges this gap and allows new business ideas models to come to life without the hundred's of thousands of dollars price tag it can take to put together all the software license and hardware required to host such solutions as there is pay on demand ethos behind cloud business models.

Testing, particularly at Scale - For businesses who are unable to, or having organisational restriction to deploying in the public cloud, Cloud providers, such as EC2, provide a fantastic way to be able to test throughput and scale. It is incredibly difficult for organisations to be able to, for example, requisition a hundred or two hundred servers to test at increased scale. Ideally this should be done early in the application lifecycle but the reality is that for many projects this either occurs late or does not occur at all, and a scaled up estimate is used. This typically leads to scaling issues once the application or service is in full production.

Reduce Administration and Operational Issues - Many organisations outsource some part of their development for either a service or an application. At some point this may need to be implemented inside the organisation and usually has to go through a sign off process (which invariably is complex and time consuming, as well as expensive). More organisations are looking at providing service interfaces that can be used as an entry point into their applications and services but in which the outsource application or service is hosted in the cloud. Not all applications and service fit this model but it's clear many organisations will see the current economic crisis as an opportunity to test this model.

Provide burst capabilities - To handle spikes and bursts. The ability to bring on servers that exist in the cloud to help out when needed is now very much a reality and it helps save money by preventing over-provisioning and still having the operational capacity to handle these peaks.

It's Cheaper - Simply put it can be cheaper deploying applications and services using the cloud than it is building and hosting them in a data center. There are no upfront costs, everything is usage based and the pay per use model enables organisation to move costs from CapEx to OpeX.

All organisations need to reduce costs, but not reduce quality or services, during the current economic crisis so this is proving an apt time to test this model. Fundamentally, Cloud Computing has the potential to change IT resources from something that we buy and operate ourselves to something that is operated externally to the organisation.

THE ECONOMICS OF CLOUD

There are many debates about the economics of cloud. In this section we look at some of the realities of cloud cost benefit models and will provide you information that you can use to make a decision for your organisation. Of course the hardest part when comparing internal costs and SaaS is figuring out what to include and what not to include in any comparative example. I suspect many organisations don't actually know the real costs, of running a Data center for example. In the example below we have excludes personnel costs, property costs (rental and/or taxes) and any inclusion of them, if the costs are know, only makes the SaaS proposition more financially compelling.

Most importantly, Cloud moves costs from a CAPEX model to an OPEX model. A capital expenditure is incurred when a business spends money either to buy fixed assets or to add to the value of an existing fixed asset with a useful life that extends beyond the taxable year. Operating Expenditure is an on-going cost for running a product, business, or system. The simple difference is rather than accruing hardware and software costs immediately and having ongoing operating costs for rent, power, heat, light etc the hardware, software, rent, power heat, light etc **all become ongoing operating costs.**

This can have several advantages:

❑ Increased cash flow.

❑ Ability to "average" into a project i.e. given that there are well known statistics that many projects can fail or be dropped. The ability to pay on demand can result in less wasted cash and less "shelf ware".

❑ Over a fixed period the Cloud Computing approach can prove to be cheaper than the alternative.

❑ In the past a company really only had two choices when it came to a new application or service build. Either own or lease the equipment and design/build it in-house or choose a managed service provider to outsource to. Cloud adds a third option that has no setup costs other than time, and in which capacity can be added on demand relatively easily and cheaply.

❑ Time to market. The ability to execute immediately instead of waiting for organisational hardware sign off, software sign off etc can significantly increase time to market.

❑ Ability to save Operational costs by scaling on demand. For example Amazon EC2 enables you to increase or decrease capacity within minutes. You can commission up to 100 server instances simultaneously. As this is all controlled with the Amazon web service APIs, applications can automatically scale up and down depending on what is needed.

What about the real economics of cloud? It is often said that using the cloud is cheaper. Of course this is going to be true in certain cases but in every case? let's drill down on this claim a little more. In a recent blog, a Microsoft employee shared some information about the costs to run a 50,000 node data center[86]. The summary of these costs is outlined in figure 26 below.

Having a 50,000 node data center may not be unusual for an enterprise organisation, but the interesting statistic fro this is the monthly cost of running a single server which we can establish from these numbers as being $112,42.

It's not clear from the data what types of server this represents or whether the server has an OS pre-loaded, but it gives a reasonable, if imprecise, indicator of the monthly net cost of running a server. We could expect this net cost to be multiplied by a factor of 4 to 5 times if the server were to be offered to a consumer.

86

http://perspectives.mvdirona.com/2008/11/28/CostOfPowerInLargeScal eDataCenters.aspx

Assumptions

Cost of power ($/kwh):	$0.07	
Cost of Facility ($):	$200,000,000.00	
Facilities Amortization:	180	(15 years)
Number of Servers:	50,000.00	
Cost/Server ($)	$2,000.00	
Server Amortization (months)	36	(3 years)
Size of Facility (Critical Load MW):	15,000,000.00	(15MW)
Annual Cost of Money (%):	5%	
Average Power Usage (%):	80%	(Average % of provisioned power used)
Power Usage Effectiveness	1.7	
Power and Cooling Infrastrucure (%)	82%	(% of infrastructure that is power & cooling)
Network egress charges not included (workload dependent)		

Calculations

Infrastructure	$1,581,587	[=-PMT(CostOfMoney/12,FacilityAmortization,FacilityCost,0)]
Servers	$2,997,090	[=-PMT(CostOfMoney/12, ServerAmortization, ServerCount*ServerCost, 0)]
Power & Cooling Infrastructure	$1,296,902	[=InfrastructureMonthly*PowerAndCoolikngInfrastructurePercentage]
Power	$1,042,440	[=MegaWattsCriticalLoad*AveragePowerUsage/1000*PUE*PowerCost*24*365/12
Other Infrastructure	$284,686	[=+InfrastructureMonthly-PowerAndCoolingInfrastructureMonthly]
Full burdened Power	$2,339,342	[=+PowerAndCoolingInfrastructureMonthly+PowerMonthly]
Total:	$5,621,117	

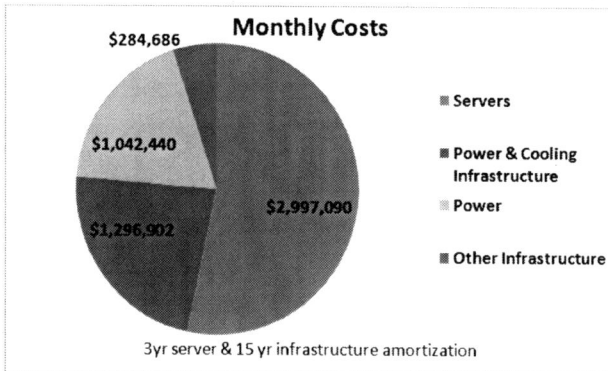

Monthly Costs

$284,686

$1,042,440

$1,296,902

$2,997,090

- Servers
- Power & Cooling Infrastructure
- Power
- Other Infrastructure

3yr server & 15 yr infrastructure amortization

Figure 27 - Data Center Costs

We can compare this with Amazon EC2 and the retail costs of running a cloud server. EC2 pricing starts for what Amazon call a small instance. A small instance is equivalent to a single AMD 1.2 Ghz and pricing is:

10cents/h. 0.1 * 24 * 30 = $72/month + bandwidth + storage

A small instance is probably not equivalent to our data center server. This is likely to be a large EC2 instance i.e. a 1 CPU 4 core machine. Pricing for this is:

80c/h. 0.8 * 24 * 30 = $576/month + bandwidth + storage

This is 5 times the estimated cost of running a 50,000 node data center, so I'd say given margins for error in estimation and Retail Cost V Net Cost, this about works out i.e. Cloud users pay a retail cost for being able to use Cloud server. It is not cheaper necessarily than data center costs.

It's not a like for like comparison but it shows that using Amazon probably stacks up well for infrastructure pricing compared to the alternative of using in-house servers.

Infrastructure is only one of the costs, software adds additional costs. Open source offers one way to reduce costs but it does not suit all needs. Third party software comes with a variety of price-tags. Let us take for example GigaSpaces who have recently announced a subscription based pricing model for their software alongside the standard perpetual licence model.

Assume we want to purchase a configuration using GigaSpaces on 4*4 core server instances. If we were to take a subscription of GigaSpaces to be used in-house then this would be this would be:

GigaSpaces subscription cost:

> $7500 per cpu per year

For 4 * 4 core servers this would be equivalent of 8 cpu's[87] or $60,000 per year.[88]

Lets compare this to using GigaSpaces on EC2. One EC2 instance is equal to 1.2 GHz AMD CPU

Using 4 extra large EC2 instances would gives 4 EC2 compute units (2 cores and 2 instances).

---

[87] GigaSpaces treat a 4 core server as 2 cpu's

[88] You can validate this at gigaspaces.com/licensing

The charge for each large GigaSpaces instance is .80 cents per hour. For a year this works out as:

$$\$1.6 *7 *24 = \$268.8 \text{ for 1 week}$$

or $13977.60 per year per EC2 instance

for 4 large instances this is:

$$13977.6 *4 = \$55910.4$$

The in-house subscription cost has support built in whereas there is a $5000 charge for the equivalent Gold support for Cloud.

This makes deploying to the cloud using subscription and deploying internally using subscription costs approximately the same.

Again it seems that using the Cloud is not necessarily cheaper. Except that there is one aspect of the equation that has not been factored in yet - the utility compute or compute on demand model. In this model you only pay for what you use and so you need to factor in a utilisation factor into your costs (which is unlikely to be 100% - the assumption in the fully owned solution). In fact using the Cloud can work out much cheaper because:

❏ During some parts of the year the business may require less hardware. This means not only less hardware but also less software, giving a two-fold cost saving

❏ Internal resources cost 100%, 100% of the time, whether they are being used or not.

❏ If the need for the hardware or software for an application is shorter than expected, it can be turned off for instant cost savings.

❏ There is no need to design and buy to support the peak loads. If demand is not what was anticipated then it is easy to scale down again resulting instant cost savings

❑ There is no initial investment required – this can be incredibly attractive on its own.

❑ Ultimately it is a trade off. It is important to consider security, latency and costs implications (see the next section on cloud best practice) before making a choice as to whether the cloud makes sense for you and your organization.

CLOUD BEST PRACTICE – WHAT TO BE AWARE OF

Some of the key things to think about when putting your application on the cloud are discussed in this section. Cloud computing is relatively new, and best practice is still being established. However we can learn from earlier technologies and concepts such as utility compute, SaaS, outsourcing and even internal enterprise data center management, as well as from experience with vendors such as Amazon and FlexiScale.

Licensing: If you are using the cloud for spikes or overspill make sure that the products you want to use in the cloud can be used in this way. Certain products restrict their licenses to be used from a cloud perspective. This is especially true of commercial Grid, HPC or DataGrid vendors.

Data transfer costs: When using a provider like Amazon with a detailed cost model, make sure that any data transfers are internal to the provider network rather than external. In the case of Amazon, internal traffic is free but you will be charged for any traffic over the external IP addresses.

Latency: If you have low latency requirements then the Cloud may not be the best environment to achieve this. If you are trying to run an ERP or some such system in the cloud then the latency may be good enough but if you are trying to run a binary or FX Exchange then of course the latency requirements are very different and more stringent. It is essential to make sure you understand the performance requirements of your application and have a clear understanding of what is deemed business critical.

One Grid vendor who had focused on attacking low latency in the cloud is GigaSpaces[89] and so if you require cloud low latency then these are one of the companies you should evaluate. Also for processing distributed data loads there is the map reduce pattern and Hadoop. These type of architectures eliminating the boundaries created by scale-out database based approaches.

State: Check whether your cloud infrastructure providers have persistence. When an application is brought down and then back up all local changes will be wiped and you start with a blank slate. This obviously has ramifications with instances that need to store user or application state. To combat this on their platform Amazon recently announced EC2 persistent storage in which data can remain linked to a specific computing instance. You should ensure you understand the state limitations of any Cloud Computing platform that you work with.

Data Regulations: If you are storing data in the cloud you may be breaching data laws depending where your data is stored i.e. which country or continent. To combat this Amazon S3 now supports location constraints, which allow you to specify where in the world to store data for a bucket and provides a new API to retrieve the location constraint for an existing bucket. However if you are using another cloud provider you should check where you data is stored.

Dependencies: Be aware of dependencies of service providers. If service 'y' is dependant on 'x' then if you subscribe to service 'y' and service 'x' goes down you lose your service. Always

---

[89] http://blog.gigaspaces.com/2008/11/07/scaling-the-web-layer-%E2%80%93-the-web-container-benchmark/

check any dependencies when you are using a cloud service.

Standardisation: A major issue with current cloud computing platforms is that there is no standardisation of the APIs and platform technologies that underpin the services provided. Although this represents a lack of maturity you need to consider how locked in you are when considering a Cloud platform or migrating between cloud computing platforms will be very difficult if not impossible. This may not be an issue if your supplier is IBM and always likely to be IBM, but it will be an issue if you are just dipping your toe in the water and discover that other platforms are better suited to your needs.

Security: Lack of security or apparent lack of security is one of the perceived major drawbacks of working with Cloud platform and Cloud technology. When moving sensitive data about or storing it in public cloud it should be encrypted. And it is important to consider a secure ID mechanism for authentication and authorisation for services. As with normal enterprise infrastructures only open the ports needed and consider installing a host based intrusion detection systems such as OSSEC.[90] The advantage of working with an enterprise Cloud provider, such as IBM or Sun is that many of these security optimisations are already taken care of.

Compliance: Regulatory controls mean that certain applications may not be able to deployed in the Cloud. For example the US *Patriot Act* could have very serious consequences for non-US firms considering U.S. hosted cloud providers. Be aware that often cloud computing platforms are made up of components from a variety of vendors who may themselves provide computing in a variety of legal jurisdictions. Be very aware of the dependencies and ensure you factor this into any operational risk management assessment.

---

[90] http://www.ossec.net/

Quality of service: You will need to ensure that the behaviour and effectiveness of the cloud application that you implement can be measured and tracked both to meet existing or new Service Level agreements. We have discussed some of the tools that come with this option built in (GigaSpaces) and other tools that provide functionality that enable you to use this with your Cloud Architecture (RightScale, Scalr etc). Achieving Quality of Service will encompass scaling, reliability, service fluidity, monitoring, management and system performance.

System hardening: Like all enterprise application infrastructures you need to harden the system so that it is secure, robust, and achieves the necessary functional requirements that you need. It is beyond the scope of this book to look at each cloud platform vendor and suggest hardening techniques, however we can give an example using Amazon EC2.

System hardening guidelines – EC2

- ❑ Ensure system key is encrypted at start-up
- ❑ Ensure you plan for load balancing in case an instance goes down
- ❑ Test or emulate the performance of applications deployed to the cloud in all geographies where you plan to deploy them. The latency could vary greatly for each.
- ❑ Never ever allow password base authentication for shell access.
- ❑ Run only one service per EC2 instance
- ❑ Encrypt all network traffic
- ❑ Encrypt everything stored on S3
- ❑ Encrypt file systems for Block devices
- ❑ Open only minimum required ports
- ❑ Include no authentication information in any AMI images
- ❑ Take advantage of system hardening tools
- ❑ Don't allows any decryption keys into the cloud
- ❑ Install host based intrusion detection system
- ❑ Regularly backup Amazon instance and store securely
- ❑ Design in a way you can issue security patches to AMI instances

Summary

Cloud Computing is still maturing, currently being at the early adopter stage.

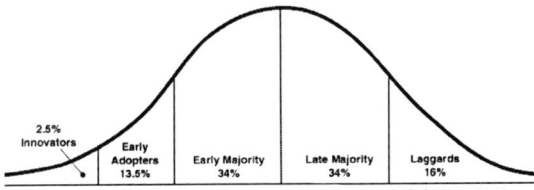

This view is echoed by analyst's such as Gartner who view Cloud as an emerging technology and warns that it could be "many years" before this is fully mature."[91]

However, organisations that use Grid and HPC, driven by the need to use of such technologies, are often seen as innovators and early adopters For those interested in Grid and HPC the Cloud presents a unique opportunity, especially in the current economic downturn, to leverage platforms, tools and services to achieve business goals whilst observing economic constraints.

Many commercial and open source Grid and HPC platforms can be used in the Cloud, and there are many more being released every day, and of course if the one you want is not available, as long as the licensing permits, it is straightforward to implement.

The use of consumer clouds for all types of HPC performance cannot be considered mature. For being able to run Hadoop and Erlang, and taking advantage of product such as DataSynapse and GigaSpaces there have undoubtedly have been major success stories.

For academic and scientific projects studies have shown that there is a performance gap not only in the MPI performance of distributed-memory parallel programs but also in the single compute node OpenMP performance for shared-memory parallel programs[92].

For those class of companies looking to use cloud computing for HPC and Grid there are some exciting consumer vendor offerings on cloud such as EC2. For those looking for a more narrow focus on HPC in the cloud they should investigate HPC cloud companies such as Parabon.

---

[91] http://www.byteandswitch.com/document.asp?doc_id=157732
[92] http://www.usenix.org/publications/login/2008-10/openpdfs/walker.pdf

Glossary

Every field has its own register, its own set of language and shared terms. It is very difficult when writing about a field to avoid using these terms, and in a new and emerging field it is common for there to be more than one meaning for single term. Of course, most of the very specific terms used here are defined in the text, and you can look in the index to find them, but there are a set of ancillary terms which are required to understand the technology but which are not directly addressed here. Knowledge of them is assumed.

However to help in ensuring a baseline of definitions and to ensure that there is adequate explanation of terms used in the text we have included this glossary which we hope you find not only useful for navigating this text but also in general as you continue to explore the field.

2PC – Two Phase Commit – as applied to transactions.

ACID – Atomicity, Consistency, Isolation, Durability – as applied to transactions

AMI – Amazon Machine Image

API – Application Programming Interface. An interface for building applications

AWS – Amazon Web Services

CAPEX – Capital Expenditure is the cost of developing or providing non-consumable parts for the product or system

CRUD – Create, Read, Update, Delete, as applied to Databases or persistent storage

EC2 – Amazon Elastic Compute Cloud

ESB – Enterprise Service Bus

ECU – EC2 Compute Unit

Hashmap (Map) interface – A structure that lets you store and look up values by a named key.

Hibernate- An open source java persistence framework

HA – High Availability (also known as five 9's – 99.999% availability of service)

IMDG – In Memory Data Grid

J2EE – Java 2 Enterprise Edition - designed for the large scale compute environment.

JMS – Java Messaging Service. This is an API and implementation that supports messaging through a common interface to standard protocols.

JDBC – Java Database Connectivity. A set of libraries for iconsistent access to databases via Java.

LRU – Least Recently Used

Multitenancy – Refers to instances in the provision of Software as a Service in which a single instance of the software runs on vendor's servers, serving multiple client organizations (tenants).

Multi instance - Refers to instances in the provision of Software as a Service in which separate software instances (or hardware systems) are set up for different client organizations.

NAS – Network Attached Storage

OEM – This actually stands for Original Equipment Manufacturer, and originally referred to a company that produced hardware to be sold under another company's name. Its use has now widened to apply to both software and hardware.

OPEX – Operating Expenditure is an on-going cost for running a product, business, or system.

POJO – Plain Old Java Objects. This is used to emphasise that this is any Java object and in particular not an Enterprise Java Bean (EJB)

QOS – Quality of Service

REST – REpresentational State Transfer. A model for web services based upon HTTP. The aim of REST is to simplify access to web services by removing the need for SOAP and UDDI and giving responsibility for function and interface to the service itself, which can be accessed using simple PUT and GET HTTP requests.

ROA – Return on Asset

S3 – Amazon S3 an online storage web service offered by Amazon Web Services.

SaaS – Software as a Service.

SAN – Storage Area Network

SLA – Service Level Agreement

SOA – Service Oriented Architecture

SBA – Space Based Architecture. A term coined by GigaSpaces for its architectural approach to Middleware

SEDA- Staged Event Driven Architecture. A robust, high performance, multithreaded, queue based, platform for internet services. Now underlying some open source ESB's and Cache implementations.

SimpleDB - Amazon SimpleDB is a distributed database believed to be written in Erlang by Amazon.com.

SOA – Service Oriented Architecture. Each component in an architecture is defined by what it does and how you connect to it. This creates a loosely coupled, service driven architecture. Usually Web services are used as the mechanism to connect and communicate between the components.

SOAP – Simple Object Access Protocol is the standard for web service based upon WSDL and UDDI.

Spring – The Spring framework provides an open source lightweight container for Java development

SQS - Amazon Simple Queue Service is a messaging service provided by Amazon.com.

TCO – Total Cost of Ownership

WSDL – Web Service Description Language. A general purpose language for defining interfaces, protocol and services available for web services

UDDI - Universal Description, Discovery and Integration. A platform independent directory in which businesses can list themselves and their available services on the Internet.

VM – Virtual Machine

VPN – Virtual Private Network

Recommended Reading

There are very few books that deal with the subjects in this book at the right level. The following are a selection of books that would be a useful follow up, although the most relevant and up to date information can be found on the web, and you can start with some of the web links below.

BOOKS

Ian Foster and Carl Kesselman (2003). *The Grid 2: Blueprint for a New Computing Infrastructure* (The Elsevier Series in Grid Computing

Michael Miller (2008) Cloud Computing: Web-Based Applications That Change the Way You Work and Collaborate Online . QUE

Chris Wolf and Erick M. Halte (2005) Virtualization: From the Desktop to the Enterprise . Apress.

Maurice Herlihy Nir Shavit (2008) The Art of Multiprocessor Programming.Morgan Kaufmann

WEBLINKS

Updates and developments in the Grid, HPC, Cloud, Virtualisation and Data Grid can be followed through this book's blog at *http://www.thesavvyguideto.com/gridblog/*

http://www.on-demandenterprise.com/. Formerly known as GridToday, this deals with news and views on virtualisation, Grid,

Cloud and Utility computing

http://thegridplace.com/ . A repository of news about grid, cloud and related topics.

http://www.theregister.co.uk/ A good place for news and views around the technology industry. Usually one of the first places you will find announcements from chip manufacturers and vendors.

http://natishalom.typepad.com/ The blog of Nati Shalom, GigaSpaces CTO

http://www.jroller.com/cpurdy/ The blog of Cameron Purdy, the founder of Tangasol, now at Oracle.

http://www.theserverside.com World renowned middlware site

http://www.infoq.com - Enterprise Development, Patterns, Design and Development.

http://www.cloudiquity.com - Blog focused on Cloud, HPC and Grid

http://www.hpcwire.com - Information *Covering the Ecosystem of High Productivity Computing*

http://news.cnet.com/8300-19413_3-240.html?tag=bc - Cloud Computing blog by James Urquhart

http://gevaperry.typepad.com/main/ - Thinking out Cloud – a Cloud related blog by Geva Perry

http://www.appistry.com/blogs/sam - Cloud Pulse Appistry Blog by Sam Charrington

http://perilsofparallel.blogspot.com/ - The Perils of Parallel, a blog about multicore, cloud computing, accelarators and virtual worlds

http://highscalability.com/ - A blog about building highly scalable websites

CLOUD / GRID RELATED MICROBLOGS

To view, type the url http://www.twitter.com/ followed by the names below:

jamesurquhart
botchagalupe
randybias
duncanjw
dberlind
acroll
onsaas
hightechdad
lancew
monadic
kentlangley
samcharrington
mrsboogie
jeffbarr
mndoci
werner
simon
tallmartin

gogrid
gigaspaces
joyent
appistry
ondemand
cloudcamp
cloudcompute
gevaperry
beaker
dekt
ymangum
paullancaster
darylplummer
elasticserver
paulretherford
boblozano
datacenter

Index

The
SavvyGuideTo

Savvy guides are aimed at getting you up to speed quickly on new ideas, technologies and concepts. We aim to create books that are accessible, clear and current.

At the Savvy Guide we are always looking for authors to join us in creating next generation books for managers and technologists of today and tomorrow.

If you are interested in working with please contact us at info@theSavvyGuideTo.com

Lightning Source UK Ltd.
Milton Keynes UK
08 December 2009

147254UK00001B/339/P

9 780955 990700